100
Japanese Dishes

100

Japanese Dishes

Edited by
Grace Teed Kent

octopus

Contents

Introduction —————————————————5
Soups & Appetizers —————————————6
Fish Dishes ————————————————14
Chicken Dishes ————————————————26
Meat Dishes ————————————————34
Vegetable Dishes ————————————————46
Rice & Noodle Dishes ——————————————54
Desserts ————————————————————58
Glossary ————————————————————62
Index ————————————————————63

NOTES
Standard spoon measurements are used in all recipes
1 tablespoon = one 15 ml spoon
1 teaspoon = one 5 ml spoon
All spoon measures are level.

For all recipes, quantities are given in metric, imperial and American measures. Follow one set of measures only, because they are not interchangeable.
Fresh herbs are used unless otherwise stated. If unobtainable, substitute a bouquet garni of the equivalent dried herbs, or use dried herbs instead but halve the quantities stated.

First published 1983 by
Octopus Books Limited
59 Grosvenor Street, London W1

© 1983 Octopus Books Limited

ISBN 0 7064 1888 3

Produced by Mandarin Publishers Ltd
22a Westlands Road
Quarry Bay, Hong Kong

Printed in Hong Kong

*Frontispiece: Oriental Steak Strips (page 36)
and Almond Creams with Apricot Sauce
(page 60)
(Photograph: US National Live Stock and
Meat Board)*

Introduction

Japan is an island country surrounded by rich fishing waters which explains the large quantity of fish, shellfish and seaweed-based products in the cuisine. Also, only a small portion of the country is suitable for farming, so the Japanese have to rely on the sea as a major source of protein.

Despite the limited area available for agriculture, there is an abundance of fruit and vegetables, including many that are distinctly Japanese. Vegetable byproducts such as those from soy beans are particularly important in Japanese cooking: almost no dish is complete without the addition of soy sauce, and tofu, or soy bean curd, is used extensively.

Although Japan shares many ingredients with neighbouring China, it has a distinctly different cuisine. Where the Chinese mix all ingredients together, the Japanese keep them separate so that each can be savoured for itself. Much Japanese food is cooked in or over water or broth, whereas the Chinese prefer stir-frying in oil. Most Japanese food is grilled, steamed or simmered and only occasionally deep-fried.

A typical Japanese lunch or dinner would consist of soup followed by several fish, chicken or meat and vegetable dishes – one steamed or barbecued, one fried and so on – served with rice and pickled vegetables or a salad. The vegetables or salad would be served in small portions, just as a taste supplement.

Japanese salads are usually composed of cooked vegetables that have been pickled or vinegared, unlike western salads made with raw ingredients. Pickling is an important way of preserving produce, and the vinegared vegetables well complement the flavours in Japanese cooking.

Sweets and fresh fruit are more often served between meals rather than as part of a meal. Such sweets as dry confectionery and cakes are made from native ingredients – rice, rice flour, red beans and seaweed gelatine.

Japanese cooking is thirst-making so tea is consumed in large quantities. The other popular drinks are rice wine, or sake, which is served warm, and beer.

The Japanese are very inventive cooks: they have done much with little. Because the fuel for cooking, which is mainly charcoal, is scarce, the emphasis is on the preparation of food so that it will require the minimum of cooking – or none at all. This has led to the characteristic attention to the presentation of food. Careful consideration is given to colour and arrangement, and to combining flavours and textures for both harmony and contrast.

The beauty of the serving and eating vessels is important, too. Many small dishes are used, rather than one large dish in the centre of the table. Two or three kinds of food may be served in the same dish, beautifully arranged to give colour and symmetry.

The western cook will enjoy preparing Japanese dishes as they are a feast for the eye as well as the palate.

Soups & Appetizers

Tempura
Fish and Vegetable Fritters

METRIC/IMPERIAL
450 g/1 lb Dublin Bay
   prawns
1 medium sweet
   potato, cut into
   5 mm/¼ inch slices
1 small aubergine, cut
   lengthways into
   5 mm/¼ inch slices
8 mange-tout
12 mushrooms,
   whole or sliced
8 spring onions,
   trimmed and
   halved
12 French or runner
   beans, cut into
   5 cm/2 inch lengths
corn oil for deep
   frying
Dipping sauce:
350 ml/12 fl oz apple
   juice or white wine
3 tablespoons soy
   sauce
50 g/2 oz white radish
   (daikon), grated
½ teaspoon ground
   ginger
2 teaspoons dry
   mustard

AMERICAN
1 lb jumbo shrimp
1 medium-size sweet
   potato, cut into
   ¼ inch slices
1 small eggplant, cut
   lengthwise into
   ¼ inch slices
8 snow peas
12 mushrooms,
   whole or sliced
8 scallions, trimmed
   and halved
12 green beans, cut
   into 2 inch lengths
corn oil for deep
   frying
Dipping sauce:
1½ cups apple juice
   or white wine
3 tablespoons soy
   sauce
¾ cup grated white
   radish (daikon)
½ teaspoon ground
   ginger
2 teaspoons dry
   mustard
Batter:
½ cup all-purpose
   flour

Batter:
50 g/2 oz plain flour
50 g/2 oz cornflour
1½ teaspoons baking
   powder
½ teaspoon salt
1 egg, lightly beaten
200 ml/⅓ pint iced
   water
Garnish:
4 tablespoons puréed
   white radish
   (daikon)
3 tablespoons grated
   fresh root ginger

½ cup cornstarch
1½ teaspoons baking
   powder
½ teaspoon salt
1 egg, lightly beaten
1 cup iced water
Garnish:
¼ cup puréed white
   radish (daikon)
3 tablespoons grated
   fresh ginger root

Peel and devein the prawns (shrimp), leaving on the last segment of the shell and the tail. Pat the prawns (shrimp) and all the vegetables dry with kitchen paper towels.

To make the dipping sauce: put all the ingredients into a saucepan and heat through, stirring well to combine. Keep warm.

To make the batter: sift the flour, cornflour (cornstarch), baking powder and salt into a bowl. Add the egg and water and stir gently to mix.

Heat the oil in a deep-fat fryer to 180°C/350°F. Dip the prawns (shrimp) and vegetables into the batter, one piece at a time, then fry, a few pieces at a time, in the oil until a light golden colour. Drain on kitchen paper towels and serve hot, on a folded napkin.

The hot dipping sauce should be poured into four individual bowls and the garnish arranged on four dishes. Each person mixes garnish into his portion of sauce, according to taste.
Serves 4
Note: other foods may be used to make the fritters. Try strips of white fish fillet, dried mushrooms, asparagus tips, slices of courgette (zucchini) and parsley sprigs.

Tempura
(Photograph: Karo Corn Syrup)

Prawns (Shrimp) with Asparagus

METRIC/IMPERIAL	AMERICAN
4-8 Dublin Bay prawns	4-8 jumbo shrimp
salt	salt
3½ tablespoons light soy sauce	3½ tablespoons light soy sauce
½ tablespoon rice wine	½ tablespoon rice wine
4-8 asparagus tips	4-8 asparagus tips
1½ tablespoons vinegar	1½ tablespoons vinegar
¼ teaspoon sugar	¼ teaspoon sugar
cayenne pepper	pinch of cayenne
little ground ginger	little ground ginger

Drop the prawns (shrimp) into boiling salted water and simmer for 5 minutes. Drain well, then peel and devein. Mix together the soy sauce, rice wine and 1 tablespoon salt in a shallow dish. Add the prawns (shrimp) and turn to coat. Leave to marinate for 20 minutes.

Meanwhile cook the asparagus in boiling water until just tender. Drain and refresh in cold running water. Pat dry with kitchen paper towels. Mix together the vinegar, sugar, ¼ teaspoon salt and a pinch of cayenne. Add the asparagus and toss to coat.

Sprinkle the prawns (shrimp) with ginger and serve with the asparagus.
Serves 4

Nuta Negi
Spring Onions (Scallions) with Miso

METRIC/IMPERIAL	AMERICAN
2 bunches of spring onions	2 bunches of scallions
3 strips of lobe leaf seaweed (optional)	3 strips of lobe leaf seaweed (optional)
15 scallops, cooked and chopped	15 scallops, cooked and chopped
Sauce:	**Sauce:**
3 tablespoons white soy bean paste	3 tablespoons white soybean paste
3 tablespoons basic stock (page 12)	3 tablespoons basic stock (page 12)
1 tablespoon rice vinegar	1 tablespoon rice vinegar
1 tablespoon water	1 tablespoon water
1 teaspoon dry mustard	1 teaspoon dry mustard

Trim the spring onions (scallions), drop into a pan of boiling water and boil for 2½ minutes. Drain well, squeezing out the excess moisture. Cut into 5 cm/2 inch lengths.

If using the lobe leaf seaweed, soak it in water to cover for 10 minutes. Drain, rinse under cold running water and drain again. Cut into thin strips.

Put all the ingredients for the sauce into a pan and cook, stirring well, for 3 minutes, or until quite thick.

Put the spring onions (scallions), lobe leaf seaweed and scallops in a mixing bowl and pour over the sauce. Fold together gently. Divide between individual serving dishes and serve at room temperature.
Serves 4

Horenso Tamago Maki
Omelet Spinach Roll

METRIC/IMPERIAL	AMERICAN
350 g/12 oz spinach	¾ lb spinach
¾ teaspoon light soy sauce	¾ teaspoon light soy sauce
2 eggs, beaten	2 eggs, beaten
pinch of salt	pinch of salt
1 teaspoon sugar	1 teaspoon sugar
oil for frying	oil for frying
light soy sauce to serve	light soy sauce to serve

Drop the spinach into boiling water and simmer for about 1½ minutes or until the leaves are wilted and bright green. Drain and rinse twice under cold water, then press the spinach to extract all excess water. Trim off any hard stalks. Sprinkle the spinach with the soy sauce. Divide into two portions and shape each into a long roll.

Mix the eggs with the salt and sugar. Coat the bottom of a 20 cm/8 inch frying pan with oil and heat. Pour in half the egg mixture and tilt the pan so that the bottom is evenly coated. Cook until the egg is set. Turn out onto a cloth.

Place one of the spinach rolls at the edge of the omelet and roll up firmly to enclose the spinach. Repeat with the remaining egg mixture and spinach roll. Cool slightly, then cut across the rolled omelets into 2.5 cm/1 inch slices. Serve cold, with light soy sauce as a dip.
Serves 4
Illustrated on page 51

Yudofu
Soy Bean Curd Fondue

METRIC/IMPERIAL	AMERICAN
1 × 5-7.5 cm/2-3 inch square of kelp seaweed	1 (2-3 inch) square of kelp seaweed
900 g/2 lb soy bean curd (tofu), each block cut into 8 pieces	2 lb soybean curd (tofu), each block cut into 8 pieces
Sauce:	**Sauce:**
120 ml/4 fl oz light soy sauce	½ cup light soy sauce
4 tablespoons basic stock (page 12)	¼ cup basic stock (page 12)
1½ tablespoons sweetened rice wine	1½ tablespoons sweetened rice wine
4-6 spring onions, finely chopped	4-6 scallions, finely chopped
little finely grated fresh root ginger	little finely grated fresh ginger root
little dried bonito fish shavings	little dried bonito fish shavings
2 sheets of dried seaweed (nori)	2 sheets of dried seaweed (nori)

First make the sauce: mix together the soy sauce, stock and rice wine and season to taste with spring onions (scallions), ginger, bonito fish and seaweed. Pour into a small pot or heatproof bowl.

Fill a fondue pot or other pan for cooking at the table with water and add the square of kelp seaweed. Bring to the boil, then remove the seaweed. Place the pot of sauce in the centre of the flavoured water to keep it hot, then add the pieces of soy bean curd, in batches, to the flavoured water and cook until just hot. Do not cook them too long or they will become hard. Dip the pieces of soy bean curd in the sauce before eating.
Serves 6

Gyoza Yaki
Fried Dumplings

METRIC/IMPERIAL	AMERICAN
3 leaves of celery or Chinese cabbage (napa)	3 leaves of celery or Chinese cabbage (napa)
225 g/8 oz minced lean pork	½ lb minced lean pork
2 spring onions, chopped	2 scallions, chopped
1 clove garlic, crushed	1 clove garlic, crushed
½ teaspoon grated fresh root ginger	½ teaspoon grated fresh ginger root
2 tablespoons light soy sauce	2 tablespoons light soy sauce
½ teaspoon salt	½ teaspoon salt
1 tablespoon sesame oil	1 tablespoon sesame oil
½ packet round gyoza skins	½ package round gyoza skins
2 tablespoons vegetable oil	2 tablespoons vegetable oil
Dipping sauce:	**Dipping sauce:**
2 tablespoons rice vinegar	2 tablespoons rice vinegar
2 tablespoons dry mustard	2 tablespoons dry mustard
2 tablespoons light soy sauce	2 tablespoons light soy sauce
pinch of monosodium glutamate (optional)	pinch of msg (optional)

Blanch the celery or cabbage leaves in boiling water for 2 minutes, then drain and squeeze out excess moisture. Mince (grind) or process coarsely, then mix with the remaining ingredients except the gyoza skins and vegetable oil. Divide the mixture between the gyoza skins and fold in half to enclose filling. Moisten the edges and press together to seal.

Heat the vegetable oil in a frying pan. Add the stuffed gyoza, overlapping them slightly in a neat pattern. Cover and cook for about 5 minutes.

Pour over enough hot water to cover the dumplings. Cover again and continue cooking until the water has evaporated.

Mix together the ingredients for the dipping sauce and serve with the dumplings.
Serves 4

Sashimi
Sliced Raw Fish

METRIC/IMPERIAL	AMERICAN
750 g/1½ lb fresh sea bass, tuna or other saltwater fish, filleted	1½ lb fresh sea bass, tuna or other saltwater fish, filleted
175 g/6 oz white radish (daikon), shredded	2 cups shredded white radish (daikon)
4-5 spring onions, shredded	4-5 scallions, shredded
few mange-tout	few snow peas
few cooked giant prawns in shell	few cooked jumbo shrimp in shell
1 tablespoon ground green horseradish (wasabi)	1 tablespoon ground green horseradish (wasabi)
lemon wedges	lemon wedges
1 tablespoon grated fresh root ginger	1 tablespoon grated fresh ginger root
light soy sauce to taste	light soy sauce to taste

Remove any skin, bones and dark sections from the fish. Cut the fish diagonally into slices 2.5 cm/1 inch long and 5 mm/¼ inch thick.

Arrange the slices of fish on a platter with the vegetables and prawns (shrimp). Mix the horseradish to a thick paste with a little water and place on the platter with lemon wedges and the ginger. Pour soy sauce into individual bowls.

Each person adds horseradish and ginger to his bowl of soy sauce, according to taste, then uses this as a dip for the fish and vegetables.
Serves 4

Ebishinjo
Shrimp Balls

METRIC/IMPERIAL	AMERICAN
450 g/1 lb shrimps, peeled	1 lb shrimp, shelled and deveined
1 small onion, very finely chopped	1 small onion, very finely chopped
1½ tablespoons cornflour	1½ tablespoons cornstarch
2 egg yolks	2 egg yolks
cornflour for coating	cornstarch for coating
oil for deep frying	oil for deep frying
lemon wedges to garnish	lemon wedges for garnish

Flatten the shrimps using the side of a flat knife, then chop the shrimps finely. Squeeze the onion in a piece of muslin (cheesecloth) to extract excess moisture. Add the onion and cornflour (cornstarch) to the shrimps and mix well. Blend in the egg yolks.

Shape the mixture into 16 balls and coat with cornflour (cornstarch), shaking off any excess. Press the balls with your thumb so that they are indented and flattened. Heat oil in a deep frying pan until it reaches 190°C/375°F. Add the shrimp balls and fry for about 2 minutes, turning once. Drain on kitchen paper towels and serve hot, garnished with lemon wedges.
Serves 4

Kyuri To Kani No Sunomono
Crab and Cucumber with Vinegar Sauce

METRIC/IMPERIAL	AMERICAN
1 × 18-20 cm/7-8 inch cucumber	1 (7-8 inch) cucumber
¼ teaspoon salt	¼ teaspoon salt
100 g/4 oz fresh crabmeat	½ cup fresh crabmeat
Sauce:	**Sauce:**
5 tablespoons rice vinegar	5 tablespoons rice vinegar
4 tablespoons sugar	¼ cup sugar
½ teaspoon salt	½ teaspoon salt
pinch of monosodium glutamate (optional)	pinch of msg (optional)
Garnish:	**Garnish:**
1 tablespoon sesame seeds, toasted	1 tablespoon sesame seeds, toasted
few strips of lemon rind	few strips of lemon rind

Score the cucumber lengthways with a cannelle knife, or a fork, then slice as thinly as possible. Sprinkle with the salt and leave for 20 minutes.

Put all the sauce ingredients in a bowl and mix well.

Squeeze the cucumber slices to extract the excess moisture. Pour over the sauce, add the crab and toss lightly together. Divide between individual serving dishes and garnish with the sesame seeds and lemon rind. Serve cold.
Serves 4

Sashimi

Dashi
Basic Stock

METRIC/IMPERIAL	AMERICAN
1 × 10 cm/4 inch square kelp seaweed	1 (4 inch) square kelp seaweed
1.2 litres/2 pints water	5 cups water
15 g/½ oz dried bonito fish, flaked	½ cup flaked dried bonito fish
1½ teaspoons salt	1½ teaspoons salt
1 teaspoon light soy sauce	1 teaspoon light soy sauce
pinch of monosodium glutamate (optional)	pinch of msg (optional)

Rinse the seaweed and wipe with a damp cloth. Put the seaweed and water in a saucepan and bring to the boil. Remove the seaweed. The stock may now be used for the delicate flavouring of soups.

If making a stronger stock to use for sauces and pan-fried dishes, add the bonito fish. Remove the pan from the heat and leave to stand for 2 minutes. Strain, then stir in the remaining ingredients.
Makes 1.2 litres/2 pints (5 cups)

Miso Shiru
Bean Soup

METRIC/IMPERIAL	AMERICAN
225 g/8 oz white soy bean paste	½ cup white soybean paste
1.2 litres/2 pints basic stock (see left)	5 cups basic stock (see left)
1 block of soy bean curd (tofu), cut into bite-size pieces	1 block of soybean curd (tofu), cut into bite-size pieces
pinch of monosodium glutamate (optional)	pinch of msg (optional)
finely shredded green part of spring onion to garnish	finely shredded green part of scallion for garnish

Put the soy bean paste and stock in a saucepan and heat gently until the paste has dissolved, stirring constantly. Bring to the boil, then add the soy bean curd and heat through.

Stir in the monosodium glutamate, if using. Pour into warmed soup bowls and garnish with spring onion (scallion). Serve hot.
Serves 4

Egg Soup

METRIC/IMPERIAL	AMERICAN
1.2 litres/2 pints basic stock (see above)	5 cups basic stock (see above)
2 teaspoons light soy sauce	2 teaspoons light soy sauce
2 teaspoons cornflour	2 teaspoons cornstarch
2 teaspoons salt	2 teaspoons salt
2 eggs	2 eggs
1 piece of root ginger, peeled and grated	1 piece of ginger root, peeled and grated
1 parsley sprig	1 parsley sprig

Bring the stock to the boil in a saucepan. Mix together the soy sauce, cornflour (cornstarch) and salt and add to the stock. Simmer, stirring, until thickened and smooth.

Beat the eggs until frothy. With a slotted spoon, spread the eggs over the surface of the simmering soup so that they float and do not sink. Add the ginger and parsley and serve.
Serves 4 to 6

White Fish Chowder

METRIC/IMPERIAL	AMERICAN
175 g/6 oz white fish fillet, skinned	6 oz white fish fillet, skinned
1 egg white	1 egg white
1.2 litres/2 pints basic stock (page 12)	5 cups basic stock (page 12)
1½ teaspoons salt	1½ teaspoons salt
pinch of monosodium glutamate (optional)	pinch of msg (optional)
1 teaspoon light soy sauce	1 teaspoon light soy sauce
225 g/8 oz spinach or cabbage, finely chopped	½ lb spinach or cabbage, minced

Pound the fish in a mortar with a pestle, then beat in the egg white, 150 ml/¼ pint (⅔ cup) of the stock, ½ teaspoon salt and the monosodium glutamate, if using. Alternatively, purée the ingredients in a blender.

Put the remaining stock in a saucepan with the soy sauce and remaining salt and bring to the boil. Add the fish mixture, stirring well, and then the spinach or cabbage. Simmer for 1 minute. Serve in covered bowls.
Serves 4 to 6

Bean Curd Soup

METRIC/IMPERIAL	AMERICAN
4 dried mushrooms, soaked in water for 30 minutes	4 dried mushrooms, soaked in water for 30 mintues
600 ml/1 pint basic stock (page 12) or strong chicken stock	2½ cups basic stock (page 12) or 2 cans (10¾ oz each) condensed chicken broth
600 ml/1 pint water	2½ cups water
2 tablespoons cornflour	2 tablespoons cornstarch
2 tablespoons light soy sauce	2 tablespoons light soy sauce
2 tablespoons sweetened rice wine or sherry	2 tablespoons sweetened rice wine or sherry
2 thin slices of root ginger	2 thin slices of ginger root
450 g/1 lb soy bean curd (tofu), diced	1 lb soy bean curd (tofu), diced

Drain the mushrooms and slice them. Place the mushrooms in a saucepan with the stock, water, cornflour (cornstarch), soy sauce, rice wine or sherry and ginger and bring to the boil, stirring constantly. Cover and simmer for 15 minutes.

Stir in the bean curd and simmer for 5 minutes longer, stirring occasionally. Discard the ginger before serving.
Serves 6 to 8

Fish Dishes

Shake No Kasuzuke
Salmon with Sake Lees

METRIC/IMPERIAL	AMERICAN
4 salmon steaks	4 salmon steaks
1½ tablespoons salt	1½ tablespoons salt
450 ml/¾ pint rice wine lees (kasu)	2 cups rice wine lees (kasu)
225 g/8 oz sugar	1 cup sugar
1 small lettuce, shredded	1 small head of lettuce, shredded
½ small white radish (daikon), puréed	½ small white radish (daikon), puréed

Sprinkle the salmon steaks on both sides with the salt. Place in a bowl, cover tightly and leave in the refrigerator for 4 days to allow the flesh of the salmon to become firm.

Drain the fish well and pat dry with kitchen paper towels. Mix together the rice wine lees and sugar and use to coat the salmon steaks on both sides. Return to the bowl, cover and keep in the refrigerator for 7 days.

Remove most of the marinade from the salmon, then cook under a preheated grill (broiler) for about 7 minutes on one side or until the fish will flake easily when tested with a fork.

Transfer the fish to a serving platter and garnish with mounds of lettuce and white radish.
Serves 4

Shio Yaki
Salt Grilled (Broiled) Fish

METRIC/IMPERIAL	AMERICAN
1 × 750 g/1½ lb mackerel or red snapper, cleaned	1 (1½ lb) mackerel or red snapper, cleaned
salt	salt
lemon wedges	lemon wedges

Remove the fish head if wished, then sprinkle the fish inside and out with salt. Leave for about 30 minutes.

Make three diagonal slashes on both sides of the fish. Cook under a preheated grill (broiler) for about 5 minutes on each side or until the flesh flakes easily when tested with a fork.

Transfer the fish to a serving platter and garnish with lemon. Serve with soy sauce.
Serves 4

Simple Marinated Fish

METRIC/IMPERIAL	AMERICAN
3 tablespoons oil	3 tablespoons oil
3 tablespoons rice vinegar	3 tablespoons rice vinegar
1 tablespoon light soy sauce	1 tablespoon light soy sauce
pepper	pepper
4 fish steaks or fillets	4 fish steaks or fillets

Mix together the oil, vinegar, soy sauce and pepper to taste in a shallow dish. Add the fish and turn to coat with the marinade. Cover and leave to marinate for about 20 minutes.

Drain the fish, reserving the marinade. Grill (broil) for about 10 minutes or until the fish will flake easily when tested with a fork. Turn and baste with the marinade occasionally.
Serves 4

Shio Yaki; Shake No Kasuzuke

15

Chiri Nabe
Fish Stew

METRIC/IMPERIAL	AMERICAN
1 × 15 cm/6 inch piece of kelp seaweed	1 (6 inch) piece of kelp seaweed
1.75 litres/3 pints water	2 quarts water
225 g/8 oz red snapper, cod or other white fish fillet, cut into serving pieces	½ lb red snapper, cod or other white fish fillet, cut into serving pieces
1 bunch of spring onions, sliced diagonally	1 bunch of scallions, sliced diagonally
4 button mushrooms	4 button mushrooms
1 block of soy bean curd (tofu), cut into 2.5 cm/1 inch cubes	1 block of soybean curd (tofu), cut into 1 inch cubes
4 large celery or Chinese cabbage leaves (napa), cut into 5 cm/2 inch pieces	4 large celery or Chinese cabbage leaves (napa), cut into 2 inch pieces
Dipping sauce:	**Dipping sauce:**
120 ml/4 fl oz light soy sauce	½ cup light soy sauce
175 ml/6 fl oz lemon juice	¾ cup lemon juice
seasoning suggestions:	seasoning suggestions:
minced spring onions	minced scallions
toasted sesame seeds	toasted sesame seeds
freshly grated root ginger	freshly grated ginger root
grated white radish (daikon)	grated white radish (daikon)
7-spice mix (shichimi)	7-spice mix (shichimi)

Rinse the kelp seaweed, wipe with a damp cloth and place in a fondue pan or electric frying pan. Add the water and bring to the boil. Add the fish and bring back to the boil. Stir in the spring onions (scallions), mushrooms, soy bean curd and celery or cabbage and bring back to the boil, stirring. The vegetables should then be crisp and tender and the fish cooked.

Mix together the soy sauce and lemon juice, then add seasoning according to taste. Divide sauce between individual dishes. Serve the fish stew hot, with the sauce and steamed rice.
Serves 4

Matsutake Dobin
Fish with Mushrooms and Chicken

METRIC/IMPERIAL	AMERICAN
4 large tree mushrooms (matsutake), chopped	4 large tree mushrooms (matsutake), chopped
1½ tablespoons rice wine	1½ tablespoons rice wine
salt	salt
100 g/4 oz white fish fillet, chopped	¼ lb white fish fillet, chopped
100 g/4 oz boned chicken breast, chopped	¼ lb boneless chicken breast, chopped
1 small bunch of watercress, chopped	1 small bunch of watercress, chopped
16 gingko nuts or chestnuts, peeled and cooked	16 gingko nuts or chestnuts, peeled and cooked
250 ml/8 fl oz basic stock (page 12)	1 cup basic stock (page 12)
1 tablespoon light soy sauce	1 tablespoon light soy sauce
1 tablespoon lemon juice	1 tablespoon lemon juice

Mix the mushrooms with the rice wine and ¼ teaspoon salt. Drain the mushrooms, reserving the liquid. Add the fish to the liquid and turn to coat. Drain the fish, reserving the liquid. Add the chicken to the liquid and turn to coat.

Divide the mushrooms, fish and chicken between four dobin or small earthenware pots (individual covered casseroles will do). Add the watercress, gingko nuts or chestnuts, stock, soy sauce and ¾ teaspoon salt. Cover and cook for 20 minutes.

To serve, pour the liquid from the dobin into a small cup for a drink. The lemon juice is served separately as a dip for the fish, chicken, and vegetables.
Serves 4

Marrow (Squash) with Fish Sauce

METRIC/IMPERIAL	AMERICAN
600 ml/1 pint basic stock (page 12)	2½ cups basic stock (page 12)
1 teaspoon salt	1 teaspoon salt
2 teaspoons light soy sauce	2 teaspoons light soy sauce
7 teaspoons sugar	7 teaspoons sugar
pinch of monosodium glutamate (optional)	pinch of msg (optional)
1 × 900 g/2 lb marrow, peeled, seeded and cut into 5 pieces	1 (2 lb) summer squash, peeled, seeded and cut into 5 pieces
225 g/8 oz white soy bean paste	½ lb white soybean paste
2 tablespoons rice wine	2 tablespoons rice wine
1 tablespoon water	1 tablespoon water
225 g/8 oz prawns, peeled and minced	½ lb small shrimp, shelled, deveined and ground

Place the stock, salt, soy sauce, 1 teaspoon sugar and the monosodium glutamate, if using, in a saucepan and bring to the boil. Add the marrow (squash), cover and simmer until just tender. Remove from the heat and leave to stand, covered, for 20 minutes.

Mix together the soy bean paste, wine, water, prawns (shrimp) and remaining sugar in another saucepan. Cook, stirring, until the prawns (shrimp) are tender.

Place the marrow (squash) on individual serving dishes and pour over the cooking liquid. Top with the prawn (shrimp) sauce.
Serves 5

Japanese Vegetables with Prawns (Shrimp)

METRIC/IMPERIAL	AMERICAN
450 g/1 lb Dublin Bay prawns	1 lb jumbo shrimp
1 × 275 g/10 oz packet frozen Japanese-style stir-fry vegetables*	1 package (10 oz) frozen Japanese-style stir-fry vegetables*
2 tablespoons oil	2 tablespoons oil
1 small clove garlic, crushed	1 small clove garlic, crushed
3 tablespoons water	3 tablespoons water

Remove the shells from the prawns (shrimp), leaving on the last shell section with the tail attached. Devein the prawns (shrimp). Make a slit in the centre of each prawn (shrimp) and push the tail through.

Remove the seasoning pouch from the vegetables. Heat the oil in a frying pan or wok. Add the garlic and vegetables and stir quickly to coat the vegetables with oil. Place the prawns (shrimp) on top. Cover and cook for 4 minutes. Uncover and sprinkle over the contents of the seasoning pouch and the water. Stir-fry for 30 seconds to mix the vegetables with the seasonings. Serve with rice.
Serves 3
*Note: if frozen Japanese-style stir-fry vegetables are not available, use Chinese-style or ordinary frozen vegetables, and season to taste with light soy sauce and sugar.

Prawns (Shrimp) with Spinach and Water Chestnuts

METRIC/IMPERIAL	AMERICAN
2 tablespoons oil	2 tablespoons oil
350 g/12 oz large prawns, peeled, deveined and halved lengthways	¾ lb jumbo shrimp, shelled, deveined and halved lengthwise
3-4 sticks celery, sliced diagonally	3-4 stalks celery, sliced diagonally
2 onions, thinly sliced into rings	2 onions, thinly sliced into rings
225 g/8 oz spinach	½ lb spinach
4 tablespoons light soy sauce	¼ cup light soy sauce
300 ml/½ pint basic stock (page 12) or chicken stock	1¼ cups basic stock (page 12) or chicken broth
2 tablespoons cornflour	2 tablespoons cornstarch
pepper	pepper
1 × 225 g/8 oz can water chestnuts, drained and sliced	1 can (8 oz) water chestnuts, drained and sliced

Heat the oil in a large frying pan or wok. Add the prawns (shrimp) and stir-fry for 1 minute or until pink. Add the celery and onions and stir-fry for 2 minutes. Lay the spinach on top, cover and cook for 1 minute.

Mix together the soy sauce, stock, cornflour (cornstarch) and pepper to taste. Add to the pan with the water chestnuts and bring to the boil, stirring. Simmer for 2 minutes or until clear and thickened. Serve hot, with rice.
Serves 6

Steamed Fish with Ginger

METRIC/IMPERIAL	AMERICAN
1.5 kg/3 lb white fish fillets, cut into serving pieces	3 lb dressed sand dabs or white fish fillets, cut into serving pieces
1 tablespoon grated fresh root ginger	1 tablespoon grated fresh ginger root
2 teaspoons salt	2 teaspoons salt
4 spring onions	4 scallions
5 tablespoons vegetable oil, warmed	⅓ cup vegetable oil, warmed
5 tablespoons light soy sauce	⅓ cup light soy sauce
spring onion tassel to garnish	scallion tassel for garnish

Rinse the fish and pat dry with kitchen paper towels. Arrange the fish on a heatproof plate and sprinkle over the ginger and salt. Place the spring onions (scallions) on top. Cover and steam over boiling water for 5 to 10 minutes or until the fish flakes easily when tested with a fork.

Remove the fish from the steamer and discard the whole spring onions (scallions). Drain any liquid from the plate. Mix together the oil and soy sauce and pour over the fish. Garnish with the spring onion (scallion) tassel and serve with steamed rice.
Serves 6

Nizakana
Braised Salmon

METRIC/IMPERIAL	AMERICAN
1 tablespoon oil	1 tablespoon oil
1 kg/2 lb salmon, cut into serving pieces	2 lb salmon, cut into serving pieces
1 onion, halved and cut into 1 cm/ ½ inch thick slices	1 onion, halved and cut into ½ inch thick slices
1½ tablespoons rice wine	1½ tablespoons rice wine
2 tablespoons water	2 tablespoons water
4 tablespoons light soy sauce	¼ cup light soy sauce
2½ tablespoons sugar	2½ tablespoons sugar
1 teaspoon grated fresh root ginger	1 teaspoon grated fresh ginger root
pinch of monosodium glutamate (optional)	pinch of msg (optional)

Heat the oil in a frying pan. Add the fish and onion. Mix together the remaining ingredients and pour into the pan.

Cover and simmer for about 10 minutes or until the fish will flake easily when tested with a fork. Serve hot.
Serves 4

Nioroshi
Fish and Soy Bean Curd

METRIC/IMPERIAL	AMERICAN
350 g/12 oz white fish fillets	¾ lb white fish fillets
cornflour for coating	cornstarch for coating
750 g/1½ lb 'silk' soy bean curd (kinugoshi), each cake cut into 4 pieces	1½ lb 'silk' soybean curd (kinugoshi), each cake cut into 4 pieces
oil for deep frying	oil for deep frying
Sauce:	**Sauce:**
600 ml/1 pint basic stock (page 12)	2½ cups basic stock (page 12)
5 tablespoons light soy sauce	5 tablespoons light soy sauce
3 tablespoons sweetened rice wine	3 tablespoons sweetened rice wine
finely grated white radish (daikon), squeezed dry	finely grated white radish (daikon), squeezed dry
Garnish:	**Garnish:**
finely chopped spring onion	finely chopped scallion
lemon slices	lemon slices

Coat the fish lightly with cornflour (cornstarch). Wrap the soy bean curd pieces in a cloth and pat lightly to remove excess moisture. Heat the oil in a deep fryer to 180°C/350°F. Fry the fish and soy bean curd pieces until golden brown and cooked through.

Meanwhile make the sauce. Place the stock, soy sauce and rice wine in a saucepan and bring to the boil. Remove from the heat and stir in the radish.

Drain the fish and soy bean curd pieces on kitchen paper towels and arrange on a plate. Pour over the sauce and garnish with spring onion (scallion) and lemon slices.
Serves 6

Steamed Fish with Ginger
(Photograph: US National Marine Fisheries Service)

Poached Fish with Vegetables

METRIC/IMPERIAL	AMERICAN
1 × 1 kg/2-2½ lb white fish such as sea bream, cleaned	1 (2-2½ lb) white fish such as sea bream, cleaned
450 ml/¾ pint water	2 cups water
4 tablespoons light soy sauce	¼ cup light soy sauce
1½ tablespoons rice wine	1½ tablespoons rice wine
100 g/4 oz peas	1 cup peas
100 g/4 oz cauliflower or cabbage, diced	1 cup diced cauliflower or cabbage

Remove the fish head. Cut the fish into three pieces lengthways from the head to tail. Pour the water into a fish kettle or large frying pan and add the soy sauce and rice wine. Bring to the boil. Add the fish pieces and simmer for 7 minutes.

Add the peas and cauliflower or cabbage and simmer for a further 5 minutes or until the fish will flake easily when tested with a fork and the vegetables are tender.
Serves 4 to 6

Clams or Mussels and Onions

METRIC/IMPERIAL	AMERICAN
350 g/12 oz small onions	¾ lb small onions
4 tablespoons soy bean paste	¼ cup soybean paste
2 tablespoons sugar	2 tablespoons sugar
2 tablespoons basic stock (page 12)	2 tablespoons basic stock (page 12)
2 tablespoons vinegar	2 tablespoons vinegar
2 dozen clams or mussels, steamed and removed from shells	2 dozen clams or mussels, steamed and shucked

Drop the onions into boiling water and simmer until just tender. Drain well.

Mix together the soy bean paste, sugar, stock and vinegar in a saucepan and heat through. Add the clams or mussels and onions and mix well. Serve in individual dishes.
Serves 4

Sakana Nitsuke
Poached Scallops

METRIC/IMPERIAL	AMERICAN
250 ml/8 fl oz light soy sauce	1 cup light soy sauce
3 tablespoons sugar	3 tablespoons sugar
2 teaspoons grated fresh root ginger	2 teaspoons grated fresh ginger root
½ teaspoon monosodium glutamate (optional)	½ teaspoon msg (optional)
450 g/1 lb scallops, quartered if large	1 lb scallops, quartered if large

Place the soy sauce, sugar, ginger and monosodium glutamate, if using, in a saucepan and bring to the boil. Add the scallops and simmer until the liquid has been absorbed. Serve hot.
Serves 4 to 6

Hamaguri Yaki
Grilled (Broiled) Clams

METRIC/IMPERIAL	AMERICAN
120 ml/4 fl oz light soy sauce	½ cup light soy sauce
120 ml/4 fl oz rice wine	½ cup rice wine
4 tablespoons condensed black bean soup	¼ cup condensed black bean soup
3 tablespoons sugar	3 tablespoons sugar
¼ teaspoon monosodium glutamate (optional)	¼ teaspoon msg (optional)
24 clams, steamed and removed from shells	24 clams, steamed and shucked
2 tablespoons oil	2 tablespoons oil

Mix together the soy sauce, wine, soup, sugar and monosodium glutamate, if using, in a saucepan. Bring to the boil, stirring. Remove from the heat.

Dip the clams in the soy sauce mixture, then arrange them in one layer on an oiled baking sheet. Grill (broil) for about 2 minutes on each side. Serve with the remaining soy sauce mixture as a dip.
Serves 4 to 6

Fish Rice

METRIC/IMPERIAL	AMERICAN
1 × 350 g/12 oz white fish, cleaned	1 (¾ lb) white fish, cleaned
1 litre/1¾ pints water	1 quart water
4 tablespoons rice wine	¼ cup rice wine
salt	salt
675 g/1½ lb medium grain rice	3½ cups medium grain rice
2 dried mushrooms, soaked in water for 30 minutes	2 dried mushrooms, soaked in water for 30 minutes
4 spinach leaves or parsley sprigs	4 spinach leaves or parsley sprigs
350 ml/12 fl oz basic stock (page 12)	1½ cups basic stock (page 12)
¼ teaspoon light soy sauce	¼ teaspoon light soy sauce
1 leek, cooked and finely chopped	1 leek, cooked and finely chopped

Cut the fish into three portions crossways. Place in a saucepan, head, bones and all, and pour over the water. Bring to the boil and simmer until the fish will flake easily when tested with a fork. Lift out the fish with a slotted spoon and flake the flesh, discarding all skin and bones. Set the fish aside.

Strain the cooking liquid and return to the pan. Stir in the rice wine and 1¼ tablespoons salt and bring to the boil. Add the rice, stir and bring back to the boil. Add the flaked fish, cover tightly and cook for about 20 minutes or until the rice is tender and has absorbed all the liquid.

Meanwhile drain the mushrooms and trim off the stems. Drop the mushrooms and spinach or parsley into boiling water and simmer until tender. Drain.

Place the basic stock in the saucepan in which the vegetables were cooked and stir in the soy sauce and ¼ teaspoon salt. Bring to the boil. Stir in the mushrooms and spinach or parsley and keep warm.

Divide the fish rice between individual bowls and pour over the stock mixture. Sprinkle the leek on top.
Serves 4 to 6

Kabuto-age
Lobster and Vegetables in 'Fried Armour'

METRIC/IMPERIAL	AMERICAN
1 lobster	1 lobster
2-3 dried Japanese mushrooms (shiitake), soaked in water for 30 minutes, drained and shredded	2-3 dried Japanese mushrooms (shiitake), soaked in water for 30 minutes, drained and shredded
1 small carrot, cut into shreds 2.5 cm/1 inch long	1 small carrot, cut into shreds 1 inch long
1-2 canned bamboo shoots, cut into 2.5 cm/1 inch strips	1-2 canned bamboo shoots, cut into 1 inch strips
1 teaspoon light soy sauce	1 teaspoon light soy sauce
1 teaspoon rice wine	1 teaspoon rice wine
½ teaspoon sugar	½ teaspoon sugar
1 tablespoon basic stock (page 12)	1 tablespoon basic stock (page 12)
1 egg	1 egg
large pinch of monosodium glutamate (optional)	⅛ teaspoon msg (optional)
pinch of salt	pinch of salt
oil for frying	oil for frying
few cooked peas	few cooked peas
4 tablespoons dry breadcrumbs	¼ cup dry bread crumbs
lemon slices to garnish	lemon slices for garnish

Place the lobster in boiling water and cook for 15 minutes or until tender. Drain and cool. Remove the meat from the body and claws, discarding the stomach, intestinal vein and lungs. Reserve the body shell. Shred the meat.

Cook the mushrooms and carrot in boiling water for 2 minutes and drain. Return the vegetables to the saucepan and add the bamboo shoots. Mix together the soy sauce, wine, sugar and stock and pour over the vegetables. Mix well to coat.

Lightly beat the egg with the monosodium glutamate, if using, and salt. Lightly oil a small frying pan, pour in the egg and stir until just scrambled. Remove from the heat and mix in the vegetables, peas and lobster meat. Pack into the lobster body shell and press the breadcrumbs over the top. Heat oil in a deep fryer to about 195°C/385°F and fry the stuffed lobster shell until golden brown and piping hot. Drain and serve garnished with lemon slices.
Serves 1

Sweet and Pungent Fish

METRIC/IMPERIAL	AMERICAN
900 g/2 lb white fish fillets, skinned and cut into serving pieces	2 lb white fish fillets, skinned and cut into serving pieces
flour for coating	flour for coating
3 tablespoons oil	3 tablespoons oil
1 medium onion, thinly sliced	1 medium-size onion, thinly sliced
½ green pepper, cored, seeded and thinly sliced	½ green pepper, seeded and thinly sliced
175 ml/6 fl oz vinegar	¾ cup vinegar
175 ml/6 fl oz water	¾ cup water
100 g/4 oz sugar	½ cup sugar
1½ teaspoons ground ginger	1½ teaspoons ground ginger
1 teaspoon salt	1 teaspoon salt

Coat the fish pieces with flour. Heat the oil in a large frying pan. Add the onion and fry until lightly browned. Remove the onion with a slotted spoon and set aside.

Add the fish to the pan and fry for 4 to 5 minutes or until golden brown on one side. Turn the fish carefully and scatter over the onion and green pepper.

Mix together the remaining ingredients and pour over the fish. Simmer for 10 to 15 minutes or until the fish flakes easily when tested with a fork.
Serves 6

Baked Fish with Eggs

METRIC/IMPERIAL	AMERICAN
75 g/3 oz white fish fillet, skinned	3 oz white fish fillet, skinned
¼ teaspoon salt	¼ teaspoon salt
3 tablespoons sugar	3 tablespoons sugar
4 eggs, beaten	4 eggs, beaten
4 tablespoons basic stock (page 12)	¼ cup basic stock (page 12)
2½ tablespoons light soy sauce	2½ tablespoons light soy sauce
1½ tablespoons rice wine	1½ tablespoons rice wine
grated white radish (daikon)	grated white radish (daikon)
ground ginger	ground ginger

Rub the fish with the salt, then mash with the sugar. Add the eggs, stock, 1½ tablespoons of the soy sauce and the rice wine. Mix well. Pour the mixture into a shallow earthenware casserole and cook in a preheated moderate oven (180°C/350°F, Gas Mark 4) for 15 to 20 minutes until omelet is set and fish cooked.

Tip the omelet onto a bamboo lattice mat or clean cloth and roll up tightly. Leave to cool, then cut across into 1 cm/½ inch slices. Mix grated radish with the remaining soy sauce and a little ginger and divide between four dishes. Dip the omelet into this sauce before eating.
Serves 4

Cod and Pineapple Kebabs

METRIC/IMPERIAL	AMERICAN
1 × 425 g/15 oz can pineapple chunks	1 can (16 oz) pineapple chunks
120 ml/4 fl oz light soy sauce	½ cup light soy sauce
4 tablespoons rice wine or dry sherry	¼ cup rice wine or dry sherry
2 tablespoons brown sugar	2 tablespoons brown sugar
1 tablespoon grated fresh root ginger	1 tablespoon grated fresh ginger root
1 teaspoon dry mustard	1 teaspoon dry mustard
1 clove garlic, crushed	1 clove garlic, crushed
900 g/2 lb cod, cut into 2.5 cm/1 inch cubes	2 lb cod, cut into 1 inch cubes
1 green pepper, cored, seeded and cut into 2.5 cm/ 1 inch squares	1 green pepper, seeded and cut into 1 inch squares

Drain the pineapple, reserving 4 tablespoons of the syrup. Mix the reserved syrup with the soy sauce, wine or sherry, sugar, ginger, mustard and garlic in a shallow dish. Add the fish cubes and turn to coat. Cover and leave to marinate in the refrigerator for at least 1 hour.

Drain the fish cubes, reserving the marinade. Thread the fish cubes, pineapple and green pepper on to skewers. Cook over charcoal or under the grill (broiler), 10 to 13 cm/4 to 5 inches from the source of heat, for 8 to 10 minutes or until the fish flakes easily when tested with a fork. Turn and baste with the marinade during cooking. Serve hot, with rice.
Serves 6

Cod and Pineapple Kebabs
(Photograph: US National Marine Fisheries
Service)

Smoked Fish Omelets

METRIC/IMPERIAL	AMERICAN
450 g/1 lb smoked fish, skinned, boned and flaked	1 lb smoked fish, skinned, boned and flaked
1 × 425 g/15 oz can bean sprouts, drained	1 can (16 oz) bean sprouts, drained
6 eggs, beaten	6 eggs, beaten
4-6 spring onions, chopped	4-6 scallions, finely chopped
pepper	pepper
oil for frying	oil for frying
1 tablespoon toasted sesame seeds	1 tablespoon toasted sesame seeds
Sauce:	**Sauce:**
2 chicken stock cubes	2 chicken bouillon cubes
½ teaspoon sugar	½ teaspoon sugar
450 ml/¾ pint boiling water	2 cups boiling water
2 tablespoons cornflour	2 tablespoons cornstarch
2 tablespoons light soy sauce	2 tablespoons light soy sauce

Mix together the fish, bean sprouts, eggs, spring onions (scallions) and pepper to taste.

Lightly oil a frying pan or griddle and heat. Pour in one-third of the fish mixture and fry for 2 to 3 minutes or until the bottom is golden brown. Carefully turn over the omelet and cook the other side for 2 to 3 minutes. Drain on kitchen paper towels and keep hot while you make two more omelets in the same way.

Dissolve the stock (bouillon) cubes and sugar in the boiling water in a saucepan. Mix the cornflour (cornstarch) with the soy sauce and add to the pan. Cook the sauce, stirring, until clear and thickened.

Pour the sauce over the omelets and sprinkle with the sesame seeds.
Serves 6

Seafood and Vegetable Salad

METRIC/IMPERIAL	AMERICAN
3 fresh Japanese mushrooms (shiitake)	3 fresh Japanese mushrooms (shiitake)
1 small lettuce, leaves cut into 2.5 cm/ 1 inch squares	1 small head of lettuce, leaves cut into 1 inch squares
3 radishes, thinly sliced	3 radishes, thinly sliced
1 cucumber, cut into thin strips 2.5 cm/ 1 inch long	1 cucumber, cut into thin strips 1 inch long
1 × 15 cm/6 inch piece of spikenard (udo), cut into 2.5 cm/ 1 inch squares (optional)	1 (6 inch) piece of spikenard (udo), cut into 1 inch squares (optional)
2 × 200 g/7 oz cans tuna fish, crabmeat or shrimps, drained and flaked	2 cans (7 oz each) tuna fish, crabmeat or shrimp, drained and flaked
Dressing:	**Dressing:**
250 ml/8 fl oz prepared vinaigrette dressing	1 cup prepared vinaigrette dressing
100 g/4 oz sesame seeds, crushed	½ cup crushed sesame seeds
few drops of light soy sauce	few drops of light soy sauce
few drops of basic stock (page 12)	few drops of basic stock (page 12)
few drops of sweetened rice wine	few drops of sweetened rice wine

Drop the mushrooms into boiling water and boil for 2 to 3 minutes. Drain and cool, then slice thinly. Place all the vegetables in cold water and leave for about 15 minutes or until crisp.

Meanwhile mix together the ingredients for the dressing.

Drain the vegetables and arrange in a serving dish. Pile the fish on top and pour over the dressing.
Serves 6

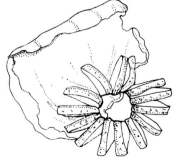

Chirashi-zushi
Tuna and Mackerel with Vegetables and Rice

METRIC/IMPERIAL	AMERICAN
2 eggs	2 eggs
salt	salt
225 g/8 oz sugar	1 cup sugar
7½ tablespoons basic stock (page 12)	7½ tablespoons basic stock (page 12)
oil for frying	oil for frying
40 g/1½ oz dried red kidney beans, soaked and cooked, or drained canned beans	⅓ cup dried red kidney beans, soaked and cooked, or drained canned beans
¼ × 200 g/7 oz can tuna fish or salmon, drained	¼ can (7 oz) tuna fish or salmon, drained
¾ teaspoon rice wine	¾ teaspoon rice wine
75 g/3 oz mackerel fillet, skinned	3 oz mackerel fillet, skinned
15 g/½ oz dried mushrooms, soaked in water for 30 minutes and drained	½ oz dried mushrooms, soaked in water for 30 minutes, and drained
40 g/1½ oz dried gourd shavings	1½ oz dried gourd shavings
15 g/½ oz soy bean curd (tofu)	½ oz soybean curd (tofu)
3½ tablespoons light soy sauce	3½ tablespoons light soy sauce
1 carrot, thinly sliced	1 carrot, thinly sliced
75 g/3 oz lotus root or chestnuts, peeled and chopped	3 oz lotus root or chestnuts, peeled and chopped
5 tablespoons vinegar	5 tablespoons vinegar
675 g/1½ lb steamed rice (page 57)	3½ cups steamed rice (page 57)
slivered red ginger root	slivered red ginger root

Beat the eggs with ⅛ teaspoon salt, ¼ teaspoon of the sugar and 1½ teaspoons of the stock. Lightly oil a frying pan and heat. Pour in the egg mixture and fry until set into an omelet. Turn on to kitchen paper towels and leave to drain. Cut into strips.

Mix the kidney beans with ¼ teaspoon salt and ¾ teaspoon of the sugar.

Flake the tuna or salmon into a small heatproof bowl. Add the rice wine, ⅛ teaspoon salt and 1 tablespoon sugar. Place the bowl in a saucepan or frying pan of boiling water and leave to heat through.

Rub 1 tablespoon of salt into the mackerel.

Cook the fish in simmering water until it will flake easily when tested. Drain well and mash.

Remove the stems from the mushrooms, then tear them into bite-size pieces. Tear the gourd shavings into bite-size pieces. Press the bean curd in a cloth to squeeze out excess moisture, then mash. Mix in ¼ cup of the stock, the soy sauce and 3½ tablespoons of the sugar.

Flavour the carrot with the remaining stock, ¼ teaspoon salt and 1 tablespoon of the sugar.

Cook the lotus roots or chestnuts in a mixture of 1 tablespoon of the vinegar, 1 tablespoon of the sugar and ¼ teaspoon salt.

Mix the rice with the remaining vinegar and sugar and 1 tablespoon salt.

Divide the rice between four serving bowls and top with the remaining ingredients in the following order: bean curd, mackerel, mushrooms, gourd shavings, lotus roots or chestnuts, carrot, kidney beans, tuna or salmon, omelet and ginger.
Serves 4

Urauchi Shiitake
Prawn (Shrimp) Stuffed Mushrooms

METRIC/IMPERIAL	AMERICAN
250 ml/8 fl oz basic stock (page 12)	1 cup basic stock (page 12)
1½ tablespoons light soy sauce	1½ tablespoons light soy sauce
1 tablespoon sugar	1 tablespoon sugar
30 dried mushrooms, soaked in water for 30 minutes	30 dried mushrooms, soaked in water for 30 minutes
350 g/12 oz cooked peeled prawns, minced	¾ lb cooked shelled shrimp, deveined and ground
1 egg white	1 egg white
1 teaspoon cornflour	1 teaspoon cornstarch
1 teaspoon salt	1 teaspoon salt
pinch of monosodium glutamate (optional)	pinch of msg (optional)
cornflour for coating	cornstarch for coating

Place the stock, soy sauce and sugar in a saucepan and bring to the boil. Remove the stems from the drained mushrooms, then add the caps to the simmering liquid. Cook until well flavoured, then drain.

Mix together the prawns (shrimp), egg white, cornflour (cornstarch), salt and monosodium glutamate, if using, to make a paste. Coat the insides of the mushroom caps lightly with cornflour (cornstarch), then stuff with the shrimp paste. Steam for 10 minutes until hot.
Serves 4 to 6

Chicken Dishes

Mizutaki
Chicken in Broth

METRIC/IMPERIAL

8 dried mushrooms,
 soaked in warm
 water for
 20 minutes
1 × 1.25 kg/2½-2¾ lb
 chicken, skinned,
 boned and cut into
 2.5 cm/1 inch cubes
1 green pepper,
 cored, seeded and
 cut into strips
½ cucumber, cut into
 strips
few carrots, sliced or
 chopped
few mange-tout
1 block of soy bean
 curd (tofu), cut into
 2.5 cm/1 inch cubes
1 medium celery or
 Chinese cabbage
 (napa), cut into
 2.5 cm/1 inch strips
few spring onions, cut
 into 5 cm/2 inch
 lengths
1 litre/1¾ pints basic
 stock (page 12)
1 tablespoon rice
 wine

AMERICAN

8 dried mushrooms,
 soaked in warm
 water for
 20 minutes
1 (2½-2¾ lb)
 broiler/fryer
 chicken, skinned,
 boned and cut into
 1 inch cubes
1 green pepper,
 seeded and cut into
 strips
½ cucumber, cut into
 strips
few carrots, sliced or
 chopped
few snow peas
1 block of soybean
 curd (tofu), cut into
 1 inch cubes
1 medium-size celery
 or Chinese cabbage
 (napa), cut into
 1 inch strips
few scallions, cut
 into 2 inch lengths
1 quart basic stock
 (page 12)
1 tablespoon rice
 wine

Sesame sauce:
1 tablespoon white
 soy bean paste
4 tablespoons sesame
 seeds, toasted and
 crushed
3 tablespoons
 sweetened rice
 wine
1 tablespoon sugar
2½ tablespoons light
 soy sauce
120 ml/4 fl oz basic
 stock (page 12)
½ teaspoon oil

Sesame sauce:
1 tablespoon white
 soybean paste
¼ cup sesame seeds,
 toasted and
 crushed
3 tablespoons
 sweetened rice
 wine
1 tablespoon sugar
2½ tablespoons light
 soy sauce
½ cup basic stock
 (page 12)
½ teaspoon oil

Drain the mushrooms, squeeze dry and discard the stems. Slice the mushroom caps into thin strips.

Arrange the chicken, vegetables and bean curd attractively on a large serving platter.

Mix together the sauce ingredients and divide between individual serving bowls.

Put the stock into a saucepan and bring to the boil. Stir in the rice wine and pour into a fondue pot placed over a spirit burner or into an electric frying pan placed in the centre of the table. Add the chicken and cook for 15 minutes.

Each person helps himself to chicken and cooks vegetables in the simmering stock as required. The sauce is used as a dip.
Serves 4

Mizutaki

Easy Chicken and Vegetable Sushi

METRIC/IMPERIAL	AMERICAN
625 g/1 lb 6 oz steamed rice (page 57)	4 cups steamed rice (page 57)
4 tablespoons seasoned rice vinegar	¼ cup seasoned rice vinegar
1 tablespoon oil	1 tablespoon oil
2 chicken breasts, skinned, boned and thinly sliced	1 whole chicken breast, skinned, boned and thinly sliced
1 carrot, thinly sliced diagonally	1 carrot, thinly sliced diagonally
12 French beans, thinly sliced diagonally	12 string beans, thinly sliced diagonally
5 mushrooms, sliced	5 mushrooms, sliced
1 teaspoon sugar	1 teaspoon sugar
3 tablespoons light soy sauce	3 tablespoons light soy sauce
1 teaspoon mono-sodium glutamate (optional)	1 teaspoon msg (optional)

Allow the rice to cool, then mix in the vinegar.

Heat the oil in a frying pan. Add the chicken and stir-fry until lightly browned. Add the carrot and beans and cook, stirring frequently, for about 10 minutes or until just tender. Stir in the mushrooms and cook for 2 minutes more. Add the sugar, soy sauce and monosodium glutamate, if using. Mix well. Remove from the heat and leave to cool, then mix in rice.
Serves 6

Chicken Oharame
Chicken Deep-Fried with Seaweed

METRIC/IMPERIAL	AMERICAN
175 g/6 oz boned chicken breast, skinned	6 oz boneless chicken breast, skinned
1 tablespoon light soy sauce	1 tablespoon light soy sauce
1 tablespoon rice wine	1 tablespoon rice wine
½ sheet of dried seaweed (nori), cut into 1 cm/½ inch wide strips	½ sheet of dried seaweed (nori), cut into ½ inch wide strips
½ egg white, lightly beaten	½ egg white, lightly beaten
oil for deep frying	oil for deep frying

Cut the chicken into strips about 5 cm × 5 mm/2 × ¼ inch. Mix the chicken strips with the soy sauce and rice wine and leave to marinate for 1 hour.

Take four or five chicken strips in one hand. With the other hand, dip one end of a seaweed strip into the egg white and wrap around the centre of the chicken strips. Continue making bundles in this way. Deep-fry in hot oil until the chicken is cooked through and tender. Drain on kitchen paper towels.
Serves 4 to 6

Chawanmushi
Hot Chicken and Egg Soup

METRIC/IMPERIAL	AMERICAN
½ chicken breast, skinned, boned and cut into 8 slices	½ chicken breast half, skinned, boned and cut into 8 slices
2 teaspoons light soy sauce	2 teaspoons light soy sauce
450 ml/¾ pint basic stock (page 12)	2 cups basic stock (page 12)
1½ teaspoons sweetened rice wine	1½ teaspoons sweetened rice wine
½ teaspoon salt	½ teaspoon salt
pinch of monosodium glutamate (optional)	pinch of msg (optional)
3 eggs, lightly beaten	3 eggs, lightly beaten
4 slices of fish cake (kamaboko)	4 slices of fish cake (kamaboko)
4 mushrooms, sliced	4 mushrooms, sliced
25 g/1 oz bamboo shoot, sliced	¼ cup sliced bamboo shoot
4 mange-tout or watercress sprigs to garnish	4 snow peas or watercress sprigs for garnish

Put the slices of chicken in a bowl, sprinkle over half the soy sauce and leave to marinate.

Meanwhile mix together the stock, rice wine, remaining soy sauce, salt, monosodium glutamate, if using, and eggs.

Divide the slices of chicken between four heatproof bowls or custard cups (or the special ceramic chawanmushi cups with lids). Add the fish cake, mushrooms and bamboo shoot equally to the bowls. Pour the egg mixture carefully over the top and garnish with mange-tout (snow peas) or watercress.

Cover with lids or foil and place in a steamer or saucepan containing about 2.5 cm/1 inch of boiling water. Cover and steam for 12 to 15 minutes or until egg mixture has set. Serve hot.
Serves 4

Chicken and Mushroom Cake

METRIC/IMPERIAL	AMERICAN
225 g/8 oz minced chicken	½ lb ground chicken
2 dried mushrooms, soaked in water for 30 minutes, drained and minced	2 dried mushrooms, soaked in water for 30 minutes, drained and minced
25 g/1 oz bamboo shoots, minced	1 oz bamboo shoots, minced
1 spring onion, minced	1 scallion, minced
1 tablespoon light soy sauce	1 tablespoon light soy sauce
1½ teaspoons rice wine	1½ teaspoons rice wine
1½ teaspoons sugar	1½ teaspoons sugar
½ teaspoon salt	½ teaspoon salt
pinch of monosodium glutamate (optional)	pinch of msg (optional)
1 egg, beaten	1 egg, beaten
poppy seeds	poppy seeds

Mix together the chicken, vegetables, soy sauce, rice wine, sugar, salt, monosodium glutamate, if using, and egg.

Form into a large square about 2 cm/¾ inch thick on a baking sheet. Sprinkle over the poppy seeds. Cook in a preheated moderate oven (180°C/350°F, Gas Mark 4) for about 30 minutes or until cooked through and golden brown. Allow to cool, then cut into 10 squares.
Serves 5

Chicken Rice

METRIC/IMPERIAL	AMERICAN
3½ tablespoons light soy sauce	3½ tablespoons light soy sauce
2 tablespoons sweetened rice wine	2 tablespoons sweetened rice wine
175 g/6 oz boned cooked chicken breast, sliced	6 oz boneless cooked chicken breast, sliced
1 litre/1¾ pints homemade chicken stock (made with the chicken carcass and giblets)	1 quart homemade chicken stock (made with the chicken carcass and giblets)
450 g/1 lb medium grain rice	3½ cups medium grain rice

Mix together the soy sauce and rice wine in a small dish. Add the chicken and turn to coat. Leave to marinate for 15 to 20 minutes. Drain the chicken, reserving the marinade. Set the chicken aside.

Add the marinade to the stock and bring to the boil in a large saucepan. Add the rice, cover and cook gently for about 20 minutes or until the rice is tender and has absorbed all the liquid. Divide the rice between individual bowls and place the marinated chicken on top.
Serves 4 to 6

Oyako Domburi
Chicken and Eggs with Rice

METRIC/IMPERIAL	AMERICAN
250 ml/8 fl oz basic stock (page 12)	1 cup basic stock (page 12)
3 tablespoons light soy sauce	3 tablespoons light soy sauce
2 tablespoons rice wine	2 tablespoons rice wine
100 g/4 oz boned chicken breast, thinly sliced	½ cup thinly sliced boneless chicken breast
½ medium onion, sliced	½ medium-size onion, thinly sliced
100 g/4 oz mushrooms, sliced	1 cup sliced mushrooms
350 g/12 oz medium grain rice, cooked and hot	1½ cups medium grain rice, cooked and hot
5 eggs, lightly beaten	5 eggs, lightly beaten
pinch of monosodium glutamate (optional)	pinch of msg (optional)
few chopped spring onions to garnish	few chopped scallions for garnish

Put the stock in a saucepan and bring to the boil. Add the soy sauce, rice wine, chicken, onion and mushrooms and simmer for about 5 minutes.

Meanwhile divide the rice between four individual serving dishes. Keep hot.

Add the eggs to the saucepan and stir gently. Add the monosodium glutamate, if using, and cook gently until the eggs are half set. Pour the mixture over the hot rice and sprinkle with spring onions (scallions). Cover the bowls with lids, if possible, to keep hot and serve immediately.
Serves 4

Chicken Stuffed Cucumbers

METRIC/IMPERIAL
15 small cucumbers,
    each about 15 cm/
    6 inches long
oil for frying
225 g/8 oz minced
    chicken
1 tablespoon finely
    chopped spring
    onion
1½ tablespoons white
    sesame seeds,
    toasted
1 small red pepper,
    cored, seeded and
    minced
1½ teaspoons light
    soy sauce
1 teaspoon sugar
1½ teaspoons salt
pinch of monosodium
    glutamate (optional)
600 ml/1 pint basic
    stock (page 12)
1 tablespoon
    cornflour
1 tablespoon water

AMERICAN
15 small cucumbers,
    each about 6 inches
    long
oil for frying
½ lb ground chicken
1 tablespoon finely
    chopped scallion
1½ tablespoons white
    sesame seeds,
    toasted
1 small red pepper,
    seeded and minced
1½ teaspoons light
    soy sauce
1 teaspoon sugar
1½ teaspoons salt
pinch of msg
    (optional)
2½ cups basic stock
    (page 12)
1 tablespoon
    cornstarch
1 tablespoon water

Trim the ends off the cucumbers, then make six lengthways slits around each cucumber. Heat a little oil in a frying pan, add the cucumbers, in batches, and fry until golden but not brown. Drain on kitchen paper towels.

Mix together the chicken, spring onion (scallion), sesame seeds, red pepper, soy sauce, sugar, ½ teaspoon of the salt and the monosodium glutamate, if using. Press this mixture into the slits in the cucumbers until the cucumbers bulge. Be sure the stuffing will not fall out during cooking.

Place the stock and remaining salt in a saucepan and bring to the boil. Add the cucumbers and simmer gently for 20 to 30 minutes or until the chicken stuffing is cooked. Drain the cucumbers, reserving the cooking liquid, and place in serving dishes. Blend the cornflour (cornstarch) with the water and add to the cooking liquid. Simmer, stirring, until thickened. Pour this sauce over the cucumbers and serve.
Serves 5

Yakitori
Chicken Skewers

METRIC/IMPERIAL
4 tablespoons golden
    syrup
4 tablespoons light
    soy sauce
2 tablespoons dry
    white wine
1½ teaspoons minced
    fresh ginger root or
    ½ teaspoon ground
    ginger
1 small clove garlic,
    crushed
4 boneless chicken
    breasts, skinned
    and cut into 3.5 cm/
    1½ inch cubes

AMERICAN
¼ cup dark corn
    syrup
¼ cup light soy sauce
2 tablespoons dry
    white wine
1½ teaspoons minced
    fresh root ginger or
    ½ teaspoon ground
    ginger
1 small clove garlic,
    crushed
2 whole chicken
    breasts, boned and
    skinned, cut into
    1½ inch cubes

Mix together the syrup, soy sauce, wine, ginger and garlic in a shallow dish. Add the chicken pieces, turning to coat them well. Cover and refrigerate for several hours or overnight, turning the chicken pieces occasionally.

Choose four metal or bamboo skewers. (If using bamboo skewers, soak them in water for 15 minutes before using.) Thread the chicken on to the skewers. Place skewers on a grill (broiler) rack and cook under the grill for about 5 minutes, turning frequently and brushing with the marinade until the chicken is tender and browned.
Serves 4
Note: instead of the chicken you can use flank steak or salmon or halibut steaks which are all just as delicious with this marinade.

*Chicken, Beef and Fish Yakitori
(Photograph: Karo Corn Syrup)*

Chicken with Prawns (Shrimp) and Vegetables

METRIC/IMPERIAL
4 Dublin Bay prawns
salt
175 ml/6 fl oz basic
  stock (page 12)
3 tablespoons light
  soy sauce
3 tablespoons sugar
24 mange-tout
225 g/8 oz boned
  chicken breast,
  diced
4 tablespoons rice
  wine
450 g/1 lb fresh
  bamboo shoots
4 dried mushrooms,
  soaked in water for
  30 minutes, drained
  and chopped

AMERICAN
4 jumbo shrimp
salt
¾ cup basic stock
  (page 12)
3 tablespoons light
  soy sauce
3 tablespoons sugar
24 snow peas
½ lb boneless chicken
  breast, diced
¼ cup rice wine
1 lb fresh bamboo
  shoots
4 dried mushrooms,
  soaked in water for
  30 minutes, drained
  and chopped

Drop the prawns (shrimp) into boiling salted water and simmer until pink. Drain well, then peel and devein. Place the stock, soy sauce, sugar and 1 teaspoon salt in the saucepan and bring to the boil. Add the prawns (shrimp) and simmer for 2 minutes. Drain, reserving the liquid.

Drop the mange-tout (snow peas) into boiling salted water and simmer for 1 minute. Drain and add to the prawn (shrimp) liquid. Simmer for 1 minute longer. Drain, reserving the liquid.

Add the chicken and rice wine to the prawn (shrimp) liquid and simmer until the chicken is tender. Drain, reserving the liquid.

Add the bamboo shoots to the liquid and simmer until almost tender. Add the mushrooms and simmer with the bamboo shoots until both vegetables are tender. Return all the other ingredients to the pan and heat through.
Serves 4

Peanut Chicken

METRIC/IMPERIAL
1 egg
2 tablespoons
  cornflour
½ teaspoon
  monosodium
  glutamate (optional)
½ teaspoon salt
6 chicken breasts,
  skinned and boned
oil for deep frying
50 g/2 oz peanuts,
  chopped
1 spring onion,
  chopped
Sauce:
4 tablespoons rice
  vinegar
120 ml/4 fl oz water
4 tablespoons sugar
120 ml/4 fl oz tomato
  ketchup
2 tablespoons
  cornflour
½ teaspoon salt

AMERICAN
1 egg
2 tablespoons
  cornstarch
½ teaspoon msg
  (optional)
½ teaspoon salt
3 chicken breasts,
  split in half, skinned
  and boned
oil for deep frying
½ cup chopped
  peanuts
1 scallion, chopped
Sauce:
¼ cup rice vinegar
½ cup water
¼ cup sugar
½ cup tomato
  ketchup
2 tablespoons
  cornstarch
½ teaspoon salt

Lightly beat the egg with the cornflour (cornstarch), monosodium glutamate, if using, and salt to make a batter. Coat the chicken breasts with the batter, then deep fry until golden brown and cooked through.

Meanwhile make the sauce. Place all the ingredients in a saucepan and bring to the boil, stirring. Simmer until thickened.

Drain the chicken on kitchen paper towels and slice. Arrange on a serving dish and pour over the sauce. Sprinkle with the peanuts and spring onion (scallion).
Serves 6

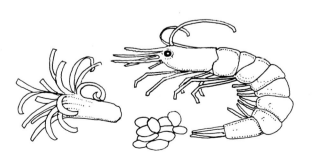

Kamo No Tsukiyaki
Braised Marinated Duck

METRIC/IMPERIAL	AMERICAN
1 × 2.5-2.75 kg/5-6 lb duck, jointed	1 (5-6 lb) duck, cut up
120 ml/4 fl oz light soy sauce	½ cup light soy sauce
450 ml/¾ pint rice wine	2 cups rice wine
1 teaspoon grated fresh root ginger	1 teaspoon grated fresh ginger root
salt and pepper	salt and pepper
½ teaspoon monosodium glutamate (optional)	½ teaspoon msg (optional)
2 tablespoons oil	2 tablespoons oil
1 large onion, sliced	1 large onion, sliced
225 g/8 oz mushrooms, sliced	½ lb mushrooms, sliced

Remove as much fat from the duck as possible. Mix together the soy sauce, rice wine, ginger, salt and pepper to taste and the monosodium glutamate, if using, in a shallow dish. Add the duck pieces and turn to coat. Leave to marinate for 4 hours or overnight, turning occasionally.

Drain the duck, reserving the marinade. Heat the oil in a flameproof casserole. Add the duck and brown on all sides. Add the onion and mushrooms and cook for a further 5 minutes. Pour off the fat from the pan and add the reserved marinade. Bring to the boil, then cover and simmer gently for 1½ hours or until the duck is very tender.
Serves 4 to 6

Marinated Chicken Legs

METRIC/IMPERIAL	AMERICAN
4 tablespoons light soy sauce	¼ cup light soy sauce
6 tablespoons sweetened rice wine	6 tablespoons sweetened rice wine
1 tablespoon white sesame seeds, toasted	1 tablespoon white sesame seeds, toasted
1 small red pepper, cored, seeded and minced	1 small red pepper, seeded and minced
1 spring onion, minced	1 scallion, minced
5 chicken legs	5 chicken legs
oil for frying	oil for frying

Mix together the soy sauce, rice wine, sesame seeds, red pepper and spring onion (scallion) in a shallow dish. Add the chicken legs and turn to coat. Leave to marinate for at least 2 hours, turning occasionally.

Lightly oil a frying pan and heat. Add the chicken legs and fry for about 15 minutes or until cooked through and golden brown on all sides. Turn and baste with the marinade from time to time.
Serves 5

Chicken Stuffed Pumpkin

METRIC/IMPERIAL	AMERICAN
1 pumpkin, about 500 g/1⅓ lb	1 pumpkin, about 1⅓ lb
salt	salt
1 square of soy bean curd (tofu)	1 square of soybean curd (tofu)
2 teaspoons sugar	2 teaspoons sugar
pinch of monosodium glutamate (optional)	pinch of msg (optional)
50 g/2 oz minced chicken	½ cup ground chicken
1 small carrot, cut into narrow strips	1 small carrot, cut into narrow strips
1 dried mushroom, soaked in water for 30 minutes, drained and shredded	1 dried mushroom, soaked in water for 30 minutes, drained and shredded
250 ml/8 fl oz basic stock (page 12)	1 cup basic stock (page 12)
1 teaspoon cornflour	1 teaspoon cornstarch

Cut off the top quarter of the pumpkin and set aside. Remove the seeds and sprinkle the inside all over with salt. Squeeze the bean curd in a piece of cloth to remove excess moisture, then mash the bean curd until smooth. Mix in the sugar, ¾ teaspoon salt and the monosodium glutamate, if using. Add the chicken, carrot and mushroom and mix well. Fill the pumpkin with this mixture. Steam the pumpkin, with its 'lid' beside it, until tender.

Place the stock, cornflour (cornstarch) and ½ teaspoon salt in a saucepan and bring to the boil, stirring. Simmer until thickened. Cover the pumpkin with its lid and pour over the sauce.
Serves 4 to 6

Meat Dishes

Sukiyaki	
Steak with Vegetables	

METRIC/IMPERIAL	AMERICAN
4 tablespoons oil	¼ cup oil
4 medium carrots, cut into thin sticks	4 medium-size carrots, cut into thin sticks
2 bunches of spring onions, cut into 2.5 cm/1 inch pieces diagonally	2 bunches of scallions, cut into 1 inch pieces diagonally
4 sticks celery, cut into 1 cm/½ inch pieces diagonally	4 stalks celery, cut into ½ inch pieces diagonally
100 g/4 oz mushrooms, sliced	1 cup sliced mushrooms
1 × 225 g/8 oz can bamboo shoots, drained and sliced	1 can (8 oz) bamboo shoots, drained and sliced
1 kg/2-2¼ lb sirloin or fillet steak, very thinly sliced	2-2¼ lb sirloin steak, very thinly sliced
1 × 75 g/3 oz can yam noodles	1 can (3 oz) yam noodles
225 g/8 oz spinach, torn into bite-size pieces	½ lb spinach, torn into bite-size pieces
4 eggs (optional)	4 eggs (optional)
Sauce:	**Sauce:**
120 ml/4 fl oz light soy sauce	½ cup light soy sauce
4 tablespoons sugar	¼ cup sugar
120 ml/4 fl oz basic stock (page 12) or chicken stock	½ cup basic stock (page 12) or 1 can (10¾ oz) condensed chicken broth
120 ml/4 fl oz sweetened rice wine	½ cup sweetened rice wine

Sukiyaki
(Photograph: Campbell Soup Company)

Mix together the ingredients for the sauce.

Heat half the oil in an electric frying pan at the table. Add half the carrots, spring onions (scallions), celery, mushrooms and bamboo shoots to the frying pan, one at a time, and fry just until tender but still crisp. Push the vegetables to one side and add half the meat. Stir-fry just until the colour changes, then stir in half the sauce. Add half the noodles and top with half the spinach. Cook for 5 minutes.

Serve the cooked sukiyaki, then cook the remaining ingredients as before. Each person may crack an egg into a separate bowl to be mixed with light soy sauce and used as a dip.
Serves 4 to 6

Niku No Miso Yaki	
Meat with Miso	

METRIC/IMPERIAL	AMERICAN
750 g/1½ lb rump steak, in one piece	1½ lb sirloin or top round steak, in one piece
4 tablespoons red soy bean paste	¼ cup red soybean paste
2 tablespoons light soy sauce	2 tablespoons light soy sauce
1 tablespoon sugar	1 tablespoon sugar
1 teaspoon grated fresh root ginger	1 teaspoon grated fresh ginger root
1 spring onion, chopped	1 scallion, chopped
2 tablespoons oil	2 tablespoons oil

Cut the meat in half lengthways, then cut into thin slices across the grain. Place the slices in a bowl with the soy bean paste, soy sauce, sugar, ginger and spring onion (scallion). Mix well and leave to marinate for 10 minutes.

Heat the oil in a frying pan. Add the meat and marinade and stir-fry for 2 minutes. Serve hot.
Serves 4

Barbecued Beef Teriyaki

METRIC/IMPERIAL	AMERICAN
4 tablespoons golden syrup	¼ cup dark corn syrup
4 tablespoons light soy sauce	¼ cup light soy sauce
2 tablespoons rice wine or dry white wine	2 tablespoons rice wine or dry white wine
½ teaspoon ground ginger, or 1½ teaspoons grated fresh root ginger	½ teaspoon ground ginger, or 1½ teaspoons grated fresh ginger root
1 small clove garlic, crushed	1 small clove garlic, crushed
500 g/1¼ lb best braising steak	1¼ lb flank steak
2 tablespoons white vinegar or lemon juice (optional)	2 tablespoons white vinegar or lemon juice (optional)

Mix together the syrup, soy sauce, wine, ginger and garlic in a shallow dish. Add the steak and turn to coat on both sides. Cover and leave to marinate for several hours or overnight.

Drain the steak, reserving the marinade. Cook the steak over charcoal, about 15 cm/ 6 inches above the coals, or under the grill (broiler), for about 8 minutes or until done to your taste. Turn once and baste occasionally with the reserved marinade.

Slice the steak diagonally and serve hot. If liked, mix the remaining marinade with the vinegar or lemon juice and heat to serve as a sauce with the steak.
Serves 3 to 4

Variation:
Fish Teriyaki – make as above, using salmon, snapper or halibut steaks instead of beef.

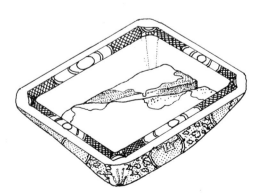

Oriental Steak Strips

METRIC/IMPERIAL	AMERICAN
2 tablespoons vegetable oil	2 tablespoons vegetable oil
900 g/2 lb braising steak, cut into strips 3 mm/⅛ inch thick and 10 cm/4 inches long	2 lb round steak, cut into strips ⅛ inch thick and 4 inches long
5 tablespoons light soy sauce	⅓ cup light soy sauce
2 teaspoons sugar	2 teaspoons sugar
1 clove garlic, crushed	1 clove garlic, crushed
pepper	pepper
3 carrots, shredded	3 carrots, shredded
2 green peppers, cored, seeded and cut into 2.5 cm/ 1 inch squares	2 green peppers, seeded and cut into 1 inch squares
8 spring onions, cut into 4 cm/1½ inch lengths	8 scallions, cut into 1½ inch lengths
225 g/8 oz mushrooms, halved	½ lb mushrooms, halved
1 × 225 g/8 oz can water chestnuts, drained and halved	1 can (8 oz) water chestnuts, drained and halved
2 tablespoons cornflour	2 tablespoons cornstarch
4 tablespoons water	¼ cup water

Heat the oil in a saucepan. Add the steak strips and brown briskly on all sides. Pour off the drippings from the pan and make up to 250 ml/ 8 fl oz with water. Mix this liquid with the soy sauce, sugar, garlic and pepper to taste. Pour back into the pan with the meat. Cover and cook gently for 45 minutes.

Add the carrots, green peppers, spring onions (scallions), mushrooms and water chestnuts and stir well. Cover and continue cooking for 15 minutes.

Dissolve the cornflour (cornstarch) in the water and add to the pan. Simmer, stirring, until the liquid is thickened. Serve hot, with rice.
Serves 6 to 8

Shabu-Shabu
Beef Fondue with Mushrooms

METRIC/IMPERIAL	AMERICAN
1 × 5-7.5 cm/2-3 inch square of kelp seaweed	1 (2-3 inch) square of kelp seaweed
900 g/2 lb rump steak, cut into paper thin slices	2 lb boneless sirloin steak, cut into paper thin slices
6 fresh Japanese mushrooms (shiitake)	6 fresh Japanese mushrooms (shiitake)
500 g/1¼ lb fresh enokidake mushrooms, trimmed and broken into small bunches	1¼ lb fresh enokidake mushrooms, trimmed and broken into small bunches
450 g/1 lb celery or Chinese cabbage (napa), cut into strips	1 lb celery or Chinese cabbage (napa), cut into strips
225 g/8 oz edible chrysanthemum leaves, thick stems removed	½ lb edible chrysanthemum leaves, thick stems removed
350 g/12 oz spring onions, cut into 2.5 cm/1 inch lengths	¾ lb scallions, cut into 1 inch lengths
750 g/1½ lb fresh egg noodles	1½ lb fresh egg noodles
Sesame sauce (goma-dare):	**Sesame sauce (goma-dare):**
225 g/8 oz white sesame seeds, toasted	1¼ cups white sesame seeds, toasted
5 tablespoons light soy sauce	5 tablespoons light soy sauce
2 tablespoons sweetened rice wine	2 tablespoons sweetened rice wine
1 tablespoon finely chopped spring onion	1 tablespoon finely chopped scallion
dash of Tabasco sauce	dash of hot pepper sauce
175 ml/6 fl oz basic stock (page 12)	¾ cup basic stock (page 12)

First make the sauce. Grind the sesame seeds in a mortar with a pestle until a flaky paste is formed, then mix in the remaining ingredients. Divide the sauce between six small bowls.

Fill a wide iron, tinned copper or brass or stainless steel pan with water and add the square of seaweed. Bring to the boil, then remove the seaweed. Place the pan over a spirit burner in the centre of the table. Pick up the beef slices with chopsticks or fondue forks and swish in the flavoured water just until the colour of the meat changes. Do not overcook. Add the vegetables in batches as you cook the meat; the shiitake mushrooms and cabbage may cook for a while, but the delicate ingredients such as the enokidake mushrooms should be in the simmering broth for only a short time. Dip the cooked meat and vegetables in the sauce before eating. Skim off the foam from the broth occasionally.

As the meat and vegetables are cooked, they will flavour the broth. When the meat and vegetables have been eaten, add the noodles to the broth and simmer until they are tender. Serve the noodles and broth as a soup.
Serves 6

Beef Teriyaki Fondue

METRIC/IMPERIAL	AMERICAN
1 × 298 g/10½ oz can condensed consommé	1 can (10½ oz) condensed consommé
4 tablespoons rice wine or dry sherry	¼ cup rice wine or dry sherry
4 tablespoons light soy sauce	¼ cup light soy sauce
½ small onion, finely chopped	½ small onion, finely chopped
1 large clove garlic, crushed	1 large clove garlic, crushed
1 tablespoon honey	1 tablespoon honey
750 g/1½ lb rump steak, cut 2.5 cm/ 1 inch thick, trimmed of all fat and sliced into very thin strips	1½ lb boneless sirloin steak, cut 1 inch thick, trimmed of all fat and sliced into very thin strips
1 tablespoon cornflour	1 tablespoon cornstarch
oil for deep frying	oil for deep frying

Mix together the consommé, wine or sherry, soy sauce, onion, garlic and honey in a shallow dish. Add the steak strips and mix well to coat. Cover and leave to marinate for at least 1 hour.

Drain the steak, reserving the marinade. Mix the marinade with the cornflour (cornstarch) in a saucepan and bring to the boil, stirring. Simmer until thickened and smooth; keep warm.

Heat the oil until very hot, then pour carefully into a fondue pot and place in the centre of the table over a spirit burner. Thread the steak strips onto fondue forks and cook in the hot oil. Serve with the sauce.
Serves 4

Beef and Wine Fondue

METRIC/IMPERIAL	AMERICAN
350 ml/12 fl oz red wine	1½ cups red wine
300 ml/½ pint beef stock	1¼ cups beef broth
1 small onion, thinly sliced	1 small onion, thinly sliced
3 parsley sprigs	3 parsley sprigs
½ teaspoon dried marjoram	½ teaspoon dried marjoram
large pinch of garlic powder	⅛ teaspoon garlic powder
½ bay leaf	½ bay leaf
salt and pepper	salt and pepper
1 kg/2-2½ lb rump steak, cut into 2.5 cm/ 1 inch cubes	2-2½ lb boneless sirloin steak, cut into 1 inch cubes
Hot and sweet sauce:	**Hot and sweet sauce:**
1 tablespoon lemon juice	1 tablespoon lemon juice
1 tablespoon dry mustard	1 tablespoon dry mustard
4 tablespoons honey	¼ cup honey
4 tablespoons apricot jam	¼ cup apricot jam
½ teaspoon salt	½ teaspoon salt
Soured cream sauce:	**Sour cream sauce:**
250 ml/8 fl oz soured cream	1 cup sour cream
2 teaspoons prepared horseradish	2 teaspoons prepared horseradish
1 teaspoon chopped parsley	1 teaspoon chopped parsley
salt and pepper	salt and pepper

Place the wine, stock (broth), onion, parsley, marjoram, garlic powder, bay leaf and salt and pepper to taste in a saucepan and bring to the boil. Simmer for 5 minutes. Remove from the heat, cover and leave to stand for 2 hours.

Meanwhile mix the ingredients for the sauces separately and place in two bowls. Cover and chill for at least 1 hour.

To serve, pour the wine mixture into a fondue pot placed over a spirit burner in the centre of the table and bring to the boil. Spear the steak cubes on fondue forks, or use chopsticks, and cook in the boiling liquid. Dip in the sauces to serve.
Serves 4 to 6

Teppanyaki
Fried Meat and Vegetables

METRIC/IMPERIAL	AMERICAN
4 sirloin steaks, cut into chunks	4 sirloin steaks, cut into chunks
8 cooked giant prawns in shell	8 cooked jumbo shrimp in shell
2 medium courgettes, cut into strips	2 medium-size zucchini, cut into strips
2 medium onions, thinly sliced	2 medium-size onions, thinly sliced
225 g/8 oz bean sprouts	4 cups bean sprouts
225 g/8 oz button mushrooms	½ lb button mushrooms
1 tablespoon oil	1 tablespoon oil
Tart sauce (ponzu):	**Tart sauce (ponzu):**
120 ml/4 fl oz light soy sauce	½ cup light soy sauce
120 ml/4 fl oz lime or lemon juice	½ cup lime or lemon juice
4 tablespoons sweetened rice wine	¼ cup sweetened rice wine
Mustard sauce (karashi jyoyu):	**Mustard sauce (karashi jyoyu):**
2 teaspoons dry mustard	2 teaspoons dry mustard
2 teaspoons hot water	2 teaspoons hot water
3 tablespoons light soy sauce	3 tablespoons light soy sauce
2 tablespoons rice vinegar	2 tablespoons rice vinegar
1 teaspoon sesame oil	1 teaspoon sesame oil

Arrange the beef, prawns (shrimp) and vegetables attractively on a large serving platter.

Mix together the ingredients for the tart sauce and pour into individual dishes. Mix together the ingredients for the mustard sauce and pour into individual dishes.

Heat an electric frying pan at the table. Add the oil, then some of the meat and prawns (shrimp). Stir-fry briskly. As the meat becomes tender, add a few vegetables and cook until they are tender but still crisp.

Serve the meat, prawns and vegetables as soon as they are ready, letting each person dip them into the sauces as more cook.
Serves 4

Note: other vegetables suitable for this dish are chopped fresh spinach, sliced pepper, mangetout (snow peas) and spring onions (scallions).

Teppanyaki

Karibayaki
Beef and Radish Juice Fondue

METRIC/IMPERIAL
750 g/1½ lb beef
  steak, cut into thin
  slices
5 spring onions, cut
  into 2.5 cm/1 inch
  lengths
350 g/12 oz bamboo
  shoots, halved and
  cut into very thin
  slices
225 g/8 oz parsley
  sprigs
225 g/8 oz aubergine,
  cut into very thin
  slices
450 g/1 lb matsutake
  mushrooms, torn
  into bite-size pieces
750 g/1½ lb white
  radish (daikon)
1½ tablespoons light
  soy sauce
crushed Japanese
  pepper
monosodium
  glutamate (optional)
75 g/3 oz beef suet
Soup stock:
light soy sauce
rice wine
sweetened rice wine
sugar

AMERICAN
1½ lb beef steak, cut
  into thin slices
5 scallions, cut into
  1 inch lengths
¾ lb bamboo shoots,
  halved and cut into
  very thin slices
½ lb parsley sprigs
½ lb eggplant, cut
  into very thin slices
1 lb matsutake
  mushrooms, torn
  into bite-size pieces
1½ lb white radish
  (daikon)
1½ tablespoons light
  soy sauce
crushed Japanese
  pepper
msg (optional)
3 oz beef suet
Soup stock:
light soy sauce
rice wine
sweetened rice wine
sugar

Arrange the steak, spring onions (scallions), bamboo shoots, parsley, aubergine (eggplant) and mushrooms on a serving plate.

Grate the radish and squeeze out the juice. Reserve 250 ml/8 fl oz of the juice and mix with the soy sauce, and pepper and monosodium glutamate (if using) to taste. Place this dip in a serving bowl.

Make a soup stock from three parts soy sauce, two parts rice wine, one part sweetened rice wine and two parts sugar. Mix well until the sugar has dissolved, then pour into a bowl.

Heat the suet in an electric frying pan in the centre of the table. Take a piece of steak or vegetable, dip it in the soup stock and place it in the frying pan. Cook until tender, then dip into the radish sauce and eat.
Serves 4 to 6

Beef Salad

METRIC/IMPERIAL
750 g/1½ lb cooked
  lean beef, cut into
  fine strips
225 g/8 oz spinach,
  torn into bite-size
  pieces
1 × 425 g/15 oz can
  bean sprouts,
  drained
1 × 225 g/8 oz can
  water chestnuts,
  drained and sliced
4-6 spring onions,
  sliced
Dressing:
2 tablespoons brown
  sugar
½ teaspoon ground
  ginger
120 ml/4 fl oz
  mayonnaise
4 tablespoons light
  soy sauce
1 tablespoon vinegar
1 tablespoon chopped
  parsley

AMERICAN
1½ lb cooked lean
  beef, cut into fine
  strips
½ lb spinach, torn
  into bite-size pieces
1 can (16 oz) bean
  sprouts, drained
1 can (8 oz) water
  chestnuts, drained
  and sliced
4-6 scallions, sliced
Dressing:
2 tablespoons brown
  sugar
½ teaspoon ground
  ginger
½ cup mayonnaise
¼ cup light soy sauce
1 tablespoon vinegar
1 tablespoon chopped
  parsley

Mix together the ingredients for the dressing. Add half the dressing to the beef strips and fold together well. Chill for at least 1 hour.

Mix the dressed beef strips with the vegetables and place in a serving dish. Serve with the remaining dressing.
Serves 6

Soboro Donburi
Beef 'Hash'

METRIC/IMPERIAL	AMERICAN
2 tablespoons oil	2 tablespoons oil
1 spring onion, minced	1 scallion, minced
1 carrot, finely chopped	1 carrot, finely chopped
75 g/3 oz minced beef	3 oz ground beef
1½ squares of soy bean curd (tofu), squeezed to remove excess moisture	1½ squares of soybean curd (tofu), squeezed to remove excess moisture
3 tablespoons light soy sauce	3 tablespoons light soy sauce
1 tablespoon sugar	1 tablespoon sugar
¾ teaspoon salt	¾ teaspoon salt
5 parsley sprigs, finely chopped	5 parsley sprigs, finely chopped
pinch of monosodium glutamate (optional)	pinch of msg (optional)
2 eggs, beaten	2 eggs, beaten

Heat the oil in a large fying pan. Add the spring onion (scallion) and carrot and fry until browned. Add the beef and fry until browned and crumbly. Stir in the bean curd, soy sauce, sugar, salt, parsley and monosodium glutamate (if using). Remove from the heat and stir for 20 to 30 seconds, then stir in the eggs. Return to the heat and cook, stirring, until the eggs are set. Serve over rice.
Serves 4 to 6

Ham with Peas

METRIC/IMPERIAL	AMERICAN
450 ml/¾ pint basic stock (page 12)	2 cups basic stock (page 12)
900 g/2 lb fresh peas, shelled	2 lb fresh peas, shelled
1½ teaspoons light soy sauce	1½ teaspoons light soy sauce
1½ teaspoons sugar	1½ teaspoons sugar
½ teaspoon salt	½ teaspoon salt
pinch of monosodium glutamate (optional)	pinch of msg (optional)
225 g/8 oz cooked ham, diced	½ lb cooked ham, diced
1 tablespoon cornflour	1 tablespoon cornstarch
2 tablespoons water	2 tablespoons water

Place the stock in a saucepan and bring to the boil. Add the peas and simmer until half cooked, then stir in the soy sauce, sugar, salt and monosodium glutamate, if using. Continue simmering until tender.

Add the ham and heat through. Dissolve the cornflour (cornstarch) in the water and add to the soup. Simmer, stirring, until thickened.
Serves 4 to 6

Ham and Cabbage Salad

METRIC/IMPERIAL	AMERICAN
900 g/2 lb cabbage, cored and finely shredded	2 lb head of cabbage, cored and finely shredded
3 tablespoons white sesame seeds, toasted	3 tablespoons white sesame seeds, toasted
4 tablespoons vinegar	¼ cup vinegar
1½ tablespoons sugar	1½ tablespoons sugar
1 teaspoon light soy sauce	1 teaspoon light soy sauce
1 teaspoon salt	1 teaspoon salt
pinch of monosodium glutamate (optional)	pinch of msg (optional)
3 slices of cooked ham, shredded	3 slices of cooked ham, shredded

Cook the cabbage in boiling water until just tender. Drain well and leave to cool.

Grind the sesame seeds in a mortar with a pestle. Add the vinegar, sugar, soy sauce, salt and monosodium glutamate, if using, and mix well. Add this dressing to the cabbage with the ham and toss together.
Serves 4 to 6

Gingered Pork Stew

METRIC/IMPERIAL	AMERICAN
1 litre/1¾ pints water	1 quart water
1 tablespoon rice wine	1 tablespoon rice wine
2 spring onions, crushed	2 scallions, crushed
15 g/½ oz fresh root ginger, crushed	½ oz fresh ginger root, crushed
350 g/12 oz pork shoulder, cut into 10 pieces	¾ lb boneless pork shoulder, cut into 10 pieces
900 g/2 lb white radish (daikon), peeled and sliced	2 lb white radish (daikon), peeled and sliced
2½ tablespoons light soy sauce	2½ tablespoons light soy sauce
1½ tablespoons sugar	1½ tablespoons sugar

Place the water, wine, onions (scallions) and ginger in a pan and bring to the boil. Add the pork and radish. Simmer gently for 1 hour.

Stir in the soy sauce and sugar and simmer until pork is tender. Serve in soup bowls. Serves 4 to 6

Buta Teriyaki
Pork Skewers

METRIC/IMPERIAL	AMERICAN
1 kg/2-2¼ lb pork fillet, thinly sliced	2-2¼ lb pork tenderloin, thinly sliced
1 teaspoon grated fresh root ginger	1 teaspoon grated fresh ginger root
1 onion, finely chopped	1 onion, finely chopped
½ teaspoon monosodium glutamate (optional)	½ teaspoon msg (optional)
5 tablespoons light soy sauce	5 tablespoons light soy sauce
4 tablespoons sugar	¼ cup sugar
4 tablespoons rice wine	¼ cup rice wine

Put all the ingredients in a bowl and mix well. Cover and leave to marinate for at least 1 hour.

Thread the pork on to four skewers, reserving the marinade. Cook under a preheated grill (broiler) or over a charcoal barbecue for 3 minutes on each side, basting occasionally with the reserved marinade. Serve hot. Serves 4

Piquant Pork and Prawns (Shrimp) with Noodles

METRIC/IMPERIAL	AMERICAN
225 g/8 oz thin wheat vermicelli	½ lb thin wheat vermicelli
1 tablespoon oil	1 tablespoon oil
1 clove garlic, crushed	1 clove garlic, crushed
1 small onion, sliced	1 small onion, sliced
225 g/8 oz lean pork, cut into strips 5 cm/ 2 inches long and 1 cm/½ inch wide	½ lb lean pork, cut into strips 2 inches long and ½ inch wide
100 g/4 oz prawns, peeled and chopped	¼ lb shrimp, shelled, deveined and chopped
salt and pepper	salt and pepper
2 tablespoons light soy sauce	2 tablespoons light soy sauce
2 tablespoons tomato ketchup	2 tablespoons tomato ketchup
1 teaspoon grated lemon rind	1 teaspoon grated lemon rind
2 tablespoons lemon juice	2 tablespoons lemon juice
4 tablespoons salted peanuts	¼ cup salted peanuts
4 tablespoons finely chopped spring onions	¼ cup finely chopped scallions
1 large orange, peeled and sliced	1 large orange, peeled and sliced
Garnish:	**Garnish:**
1 slice orange	1 slice orange
watercress	watercress

Cook the noodles in boiling water until just tender. Meanwhile heat the oil in a large frying pan. Add the garlic and fry until golden brown. Discard the garlic. To the frying pan add the onion and pork and fry until the onion is softened and the pork begins to change colour. Stir in the prawns (shrimp) and salt and pepper to taste and continue cooking, stirring constantly, for 3 minutes.

Add the soy sauce, ketchup, lemon rind and juice, peanuts, spring onions (scallions) and orange slices. Drain the noodles well and add to the pan. Continue cooking, tossing and stirring lightly, until piping hot. Garnish with orange and watercress. Serves 6

Piquant Pork and Prawns (Shrimp) with Noodles (Photograph: Sunkist Growers Inc)

Oriental Pork Strips

METRIC/IMPERIAL	AMERICAN
1 tablespoon oil	1 tablespoon oil
900 g/2 lb lean pork, cut into strips 5 mm/ ¼ inch thick and 5 cm/2 inches long	2 lb lean pork, cut into strips ¼ inch thick and 2 inches long
¼ teaspoon ground ginger	¼ teaspoon ground ginger
pinch of grated nutmeg	pinch of grated nutmeg
salt	salt
120 ml/4 fl oz plus 2 tablespoons water	½ cup plus 2 tablespoons water
2 tablespoons light soy sauce	2 tablespoons light soy sauce
2 tablespoons rice wine or dry sherry	2 tablespoons rice wine or dry sherry
2 celery sticks, sliced diagonally	2 celery stalks, sliced diagonally
1 medium onion, sliced	1 medium-size onion, sliced
100 g/4 oz mushrooms, sliced	1 cup sliced mushrooms
1 medium green pepper, cored, seeded and cut into thin strips	1 medium-size green pepper, seeded and cut into thin strips
2 teaspoons cornflour	2 teaspoons cornstarch
1 × 50 g/2 oz jar or can chopped pimento, drained	1 jar (2 oz) chopped pimiento, drained

Heat the oil in a large frying pan. Add the pork strips, in batches if necessary, and brown all over. Pour off the fat from the pan and return all the pork strips. Mix together the ginger, nutmeg and salt to taste and sprinkle over the pork. Add the 120 ml/4 fl oz (½ cup) water, the soy sauce and wine or sherry and stir well. Cover tightly and cook gently for 30 minutes.

Stir in the celery and onion. Cover again and cook for a further 10 minutes. Add the mushrooms and green pepper and continue cooking, covered, for 5 minutes or until the meat and vegetables are tender.

Dissolve the cornflour (cornstarch) in the remaining water and stir into the pan. Simmer, stirring, until thickened. Stir in the pimento and cook for a final 2 minutes.
Serves 4

Fried Pork and Apple Balls

METRIC/IMPERIAL	AMERICAN
½ dessert apple, cored and diced	½ apple, cored and diced
3 dried mushrooms, soaked in water for 30 minutes, drained and torn into tiny pieces	3 dried mushrooms, soaked in water for 30 minutes, drained and torn into tiny pieces
1 small spring onion, minced	1 small scallion, minced
1 egg	1 egg
450 g/1 lb minced pork	1 lb ground pork
1 tablespoon rice wine	1 tablespoon rice wine
1 teaspoon salt	1 teaspoon salt
pinch of monosodium glutamate (optional)	pinch of msg (optional)
oil for deep frying	oil for deep frying
lettuce leaves	lettuce leaves
Sauce:	**Sauce:**
light soy sauce	light soy sauce
vinegar	vinegar
dry mustard	dry mustard
monosodium glutamate (optional)	msg (optional)

Mix together the apple, mushrooms, spring onion (scallion), egg, pork, rice wine, salt and monosodium glutamate, if using. Shape into about 15 patties. Deep fry in oil until golden brown and cooked through. Drain on kitchen paper towels.

Serve on lettuce leaves with a sauce made of equal parts of soy sauce and vinegar seasoned to taste with mustard and monosodium glutamate, if using.
Serves 5

Tonkatsu
Pork Chops

METRIC/IMPERIAL	AMERICAN
4-6 boned loin or chump pork chops	4-6 boneless loin or butterfly pork chops
salt and pepper	salt and pepper
flour for coating	flour for coating
2 eggs, beaten	2 eggs, beaten
coarse dry breadcrumbs for coating	coarse dry bread crumbs for coating
oil for deep frying	oil for deep frying
Garnish:	**Garnish:**
finely shredded cabbage	finely shredded cabbage
parsley sprigs	parsley sprigs

Pound the pork chops with a mallet to flatten them slightly, then sprinkle on both sides with salt and pepper. Coat with flour, dip into the egg and coat with breadcrumbs.

Heat the oil in a deep-fat fryer to 180°C/350°F. Add the pork and fry for 10 minutes or until cooked through and browned on both sides. Drain on kitchen paper towels.

Cut each chop into three or four slices and reshape on a serving dish. Surround with shredded cabbage and garnish with parsley. If liked, serve with tonkatsu sauce, a commercially-prepared thick brown sauce.
Serves 4 to 6

Pork and Courgette (Zucchini) Stew

METRIC/IMPERIAL	AMERICAN
oil for frying	oil for frying
225 g/8 oz boned lean pork, cut into 2 cm/¾ inch cubes	½ lb boneless lean pork, cut into ¾ inch cubes
675 g/1½ lb courgettes, cut into 2.5 cm/1 inch cubes	1½ lb zucchini, cut into 1 inch cubes
450 ml/¾ pint basic stock (page 12)	2 cups basic stock (page 12)
pinch of monosodium glutamate (optional)	pinch of msg (optional)
salt and pepper	salt and pepper

Heat a little oil in a large frying pan. Add the pork cubes and brown on all sides. Remove from the pan.

Add the courgettes (zucchini) and brown lightly. Return the pork to the pan with the stock, monosodium glutamate, if using, and salt and pepper to taste. Bring to the boil and simmer until the pork is tender and the stock has almost evaporated.
Serves 4 to 6

Pork and Green Bean Salad

METRIC/IMPERIAL	AMERICAN
2 tablespoons white sesame seeds, toasted	2 tablespoons white sesame seeds, toasted
2 tablespoons basic stock (page 12)	2 tablespoons basic stock (page 12)
2 tablespoons sugar	2 tablespoons sugar
4 teaspoons light soy sauce	4 teaspoons light soy sauce
salt	salt
pinch of monosodium glutamate (optional)	pinch of msg (optional)
225 g/8 oz lean boned pork, cut into thin strips 5 cm/2 inches long	½ lb lean boneless pork, cut into thin strips 2 inches long
350 g/12 oz green beans	¾ lb green beans
2 squares of soy bean curd (tofu)	2 squares of soybean curd (tofu)

Crush the sesame seeds in a mortar with a pestle. Add the stock, sugar, 3 teaspoons of the soy sauce, 1½ teaspoons salt and the monosodium glutamate, if using. Mix well.

Drop the pork strips into boiling salted water and simmer until tender. Drain and cool.

Drop the beans into boiling salted water and simmer until tender. Drain and cool, then cut into 5 cm/2 inch lengths.

Squeeze the soy bean curd in a cloth to remove excess moisture. Add to the sesame seed dressing with the pork and beans and toss together. Serve on individual plates.
Serves 4

Vegetable Dishes

Harusame Soup
Spring Rain Soup

METRIC/IMPERIAL	AMERICAN
100 g/4 oz dehydrated mung bean threads (saifun) or soy bean noodles, soaked in boiling water for 30 minutes	1 cup dehydrated mung bean threads (saifun) or soybean noodles, soaked in boiling water for 30 minutes
2-3 dried mushrooms, soaked in boiling water for 20 minutes	2-3 dried mushrooms, soaked in boiling water for 20 minutes
1 litre/1¾ pints basic stock (page 12) or chicken stock	1 quart basic stock (page 12) or chicken broth
pinch of monosodium glutamate (optional)	pinch of msg (optional)
1 tablespoon rice wine	1 tablespoon rice wine
salt	salt
100 g/4 oz peeled prawns	⅔ cup shelled shrimp
6-8 mange-tout	6-8 snow peas
2 carrots, sliced or chopped	2 carrots, sliced or chopped
few cucumber strips	few cucumber strips
100 g/4 oz celery or Chinese cabbage (napa)	¼ lb celery or Chinese cabbage (napa)
few spinach leaves	few spinach leaves
Garnish:	**Garnish:**
1 teaspoon grated fresh root ginger	1 teaspoon grated fresh ginger root
1 spring onion, finely shredded	1 scallion, finely shredded
2 teaspoons puréed white radish (daikon)	2 teaspoons puréed white radish (daikon)

Drain the mung bean threads and cut into 5 cm/2 inch lengths. Drain the mushrooms, reserving the soaking liquid; cut off stems.

Put the stock in a saucepan. Carefully pour in the mushroom soaking liquid, leaving behind any sandy sediment at the bottom – this should be discarded. Bring to the boil and simmer for 2 minutes. Stir in the monosodium glutamate, if using, the rice wine and salt to taste.

Divide the liquid between four warmed soup bowls. Arrange the remaining ingredients on a serving dish, cutting the vegetables to make attractive shapes, if wished. Place the garnish ingredients on separate dishes. Each person adds ingredients and garnishes to his bowl, according to taste.
Serves 4

Sesame Spinach Salad

METRIC/IMPERIAL	AMERICAN
450 g/1 lb spinach	1 lb spinach
2 tablespoons sesame seeds	2 tablespoons sesame seeds
1 tablespoon light soy sauce	1 tablespoon light soy sauce

Cook the spinach in boiling water for 3 minutes.

Meanwhile heat the sesame seeds in a frying pan, then grind them in a mortar with a pestle. Add the soy sauce to the ground sesame seeds and mix well.

Drain the spinach, pressing to extract all excess moisture. Cut into 4 cm/1½ inch lengths. Add the sesame seed mixture and toss to coat the spinach. Serve in a shallow dish.
Serves 4

Harusame Soup

Tofu 'Steak'
Fried Soy Bean Curd

METRIC/IMPERIAL	AMERICAN
900 g/2 lb soy bean curd (tofu)	2 lb soybean curd (tofu)
oil for frying	oil for frying
2 tablespoons light soy sauce	2 tablespoons light soy sauce ∘
2 tablespoons rice wine	2 tablespoons rice wine
2 tablespoons sweetened rice wine	2 tablespoons sweetened rice wine
Garnish:	**Garnish:**
finely chopped spring onions	finely chopped scallions
finely grated fresh root ginger	finely grated fresh ginger root

Cut the soy bean curd in half lengthways, then wrap in a cloth and pat lightly to remove excess moisture. Lightly oil a large frying pan and heat. Add the soy bean curd and fry until golden brown on both sides and the heat reaches the centre.

Meanwhile place the soy sauce and wines in a saucepan and bring to the boil. Pour over the fried soy bean curd. Serve hot, garnished with spring onions (scallions) and ginger.
Serves 6

Dressed Turnips

METRIC/IMPERIAL	AMERICAN
4 small turnips	4 small white turnips
salt	salt
1 tablespoon vinegar	1 tablespoon vinegar
1 teaspoon sugar	1 teaspoon sugar
1 tablespoon sweetened rice wine	1 tablespoon sweetened rice wine
crumbled dried red pepper	dried red pepper flakes

Make two lengthways cuts in the peeled turnips at 90° angles, without cutting all the way through. Drop the turnips into boiling salted water and simmer until just tender. Drain well.

Mix together the vinegar, sugar, rice wine and 1¼ teaspoons salt and add the turnips. Stir to coat. Leave to marinate for at least 1 hour. Serve sprinkled with red pepper.
Serves 4

Hijiki To Aburage
Seaweed with Fried Bean Cake

METRIC/IMPERIAL	AMERICAN
5 tablespoons dry brown algae seaweed (hijiki)	5 tablespoons dry brown algae seaweed (hijiki)
2 fried soy bean cakes	2 fried soybean cakes
1 teaspoon oil	1 teaspoon oil
150 ml/¼ pint basic stock (page 12)	¾ cup basic stock (page 12)
1 tablespoon sweetened rice wine	1 tablespoon sweetened rice wine
2½ teaspoons sugar	2½ teaspoons sugar
2 tablespoons light soy sauce	2 tablespoons light soy sauce

Pick out as much sediment from the seaweed as possible, then soak the seaweed in cold water for 1 hour. Drain and rinse thoroughly under cold running water, making sure all the sand is removed. Drain well.

Wash the soy bean cakes in boiling water to remove excess oil, then cut lengthways into 5 mm/¼ inch slices.

Heat the oil in a frying pan. Add the seaweed and fry for about 2 minutes. Add the soy bean cake slices and stock and simmer for 5 minutes.

Stir in the remaining ingredients and simmer for 7 minutes or until the liquid has evaporated. Serve hot.
Serves 4

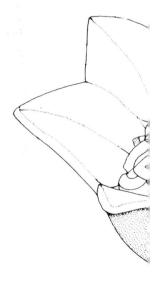

'Brown Sack' Sushi

METRIC/IMPERIAL	AMERICAN
1 × 40 g/1½ oz packet fried soy bean cake	1 package (1½ oz) fried soybean cake
250 ml/8 fl oz basic stock (page 12)	1 cup basic stock (page 12)
100 g/4 oz sugar	½ cup sugar
5 tablespoons light soy sauce	5 tablespoons light soy sauce
1 teaspoon monosodium glutamate (optional)	1 teaspoon msg (optional)
625 g/1 lb 6 oz steamed rice (page 57)	4 cups steamed rice (page 57)
4 tablespoons seasoned rice vinegar	¼ cup seasoned rice vinegar

Cut the soy bean cake in half to form the brown sacks. Drop into boiling water and boil for 2 minutes. Drain and cool, then squeeze out all excess water.

Place the stock, sugar, soy sauce and monosodium glutamate (if using) in a saucepan and bring to the boil, stirring to dissolve the sugar. Add the brown sacks and simmer gently for 20 minutes. Stir occasionally, being careful not to tear the sacks. Drain and leave to cool.

Mix together the rice and vinegar and use to stuff the brown sacks.
Serves 4 to 6

Beans or Peas with Egg

METRIC/IMPERIAL	AMERICAN
175 ml/6 fl oz basic stock (page 12)	¾ cup basic stock (page 12)
1½ tablespoons light soy sauce	1½ tablespoons light soy sauce
1½ tablespoons sugar	1½ tablespoons sugar
225 g/8 oz green beans, sliced, or peas	½ lb green beans, sliced, or peas
2 eggs, beaten	2 eggs, beaten

Place the stock, soy sauce and sugar in a saucepan and bring to the boil. Add the beans or peas and simmer until just tender. Pour over the eggs, cover and simmer gently until the eggs are just set.
Serves 4

Shimeji
Tree Oyster Mushrooms

METRIC/IMPERIAL	AMERICAN
1½ teaspoons butter	1½ teaspoons butter
1 clove garlic, crushed	1 clove garlic, crushed
225 g/8 oz fresh tree oyster mushrooms (shimeji), torn into bite-size pieces	½ lb fresh tree oyster mushrooms (shimeji), torn into bite-size pieces
1 teaspoon rice wine	1 teaspoon rice wine
3 tablespoons chicken stock	3 tablespoons chicken broth
salt and pepper	salt and pepper
pinch of monosodium glutamate (optional)	pinch of msg (optional)

Melt the butter in a frying pan. Add the garlic and stir-fry for 30 seconds, then stir in the mushrooms and rice wine. Stir-fry for 1 minute. Add the remaining ingredients and cook for 2 minutes. Serve hot, as a side dish.
Serves 4

Nasu No Karashi
Mustard-Pickled Aubergine (Eggplant)

METRIC/IMPERIAL	AMERICAN
1 medium aubergine	1 medium-size eggplant
750 ml/1¼ pints water	3 cups water
1 tablespoon salt	1 tablespoon salt
Dressing:	**Dressing:**
1 teaspoon dry mustard	1 teaspoon dry mustard
3 tablespoons light soy sauce	3 tablespoons light soy sauce
3 tablespoons sweetened rice wine	3 tablespoons sweetened rice wine
3 tablespoons sugar	3 tablespoons sugar
pinch of monosodium glutamate (optional)	pinch of msg (optional)

Cut the aubergine (eggplant) crossways into 3 mm/⅛ inch thick slices, then cut the slices into quarters. Soak in the water, with the salt added, for 1 hour.

Meanwhile mix together all the dressing ingredients.

Drain the aubergine (eggplant) and pat dry with kitchen paper towels. Arrange in a glass serving dish and pour over the dressing. Cover and chill for several hours or overnight.
Serves 4

Vegetable, Noodle and Sesame Salad

METRIC/IMPERIAL	AMERICAN
350 g/12 oz white radish (daikon), thinly sliced	¾ lb white radish (daikon), thinly sliced
salt	salt
100 g/4 oz carrots, thinly sliced	¼ lb carrots, thinly sliced
1 fried soy bean cake	1 fried soybean cake
1 packet of yam noodles (shirataki)	1 package of yam noodles (shirataki)
4 dried mushrooms, soaked in water for 30 minutes and drained	4 dried mushrooms, soaked in water for 30 minutes and drained
4 tablespoons basic stock (page 12)	¼ cup basic stock (page 12)
1 tablespoon sugar	1 tablespoon sugar
1 tablespoon light soy sauce	1 tablespoon light soy sauce
Dressing:	**Dressing:**
3 tablespoons white sesame seeds, toasted	3 tablespoons white sesame seeds, toasted
2 tablespoons vinegar	2 tablespoons vinegar
2 tablespoons sugar	2 tablespoons sugar
1 tablespoon light soy sauce	1 tablespoon light soy sauce
1½ teaspoons salt	1½ teaspoons salt

Sprinkle the radish with salt. Sprinkle the carrots with salt. Place the fried bean cake, noodles and mushrooms in a saucepan and add the stock, sugar and soy sauce. Bring to the boil and simmer until the noodles are tender.

Meanwhile drop the radish and carrots into a pan of boiling water and simmer until just tender. Drain well and cool.

Allow the noodle mixture to cool, then add the radish and carrots and mix together.

To make the dressing, pound the sesame seeds in a mortar with a pestle. Add the remaining dressing ingredients and mix well. Pour the dressing over the salad and toss to coat.
Serves 4 to 6

Horenso Tamago Maki (page 8); Nasu No Karashi in centre

Napa No Tsukemono
Cabbage Pickles

METRIC/IMPERIAL	AMERICAN
1 large head of celery or Chinese cabbage (napa), quartered	1 large head of celery or Chinese cabbage (napa), quartered
3 tablespoons sea salt	3 tablespoons sea salt
4 tablespoons raisins or chopped prunes	¼ cup raisins or chopped prunes
250 ml/8 fl oz water	1 cup water
3 dried chillies	3 dried chili peppers

Arrange the cabbage in a glass bowl, sprinkling each layer with the salt. Add the remaining ingredients and mix until the salt has dissolved. Place a saucer and weight on top of the cabbage to keep it submerged, then leave to marinate for 12 hours.

Discard the raisins or prunes and chillies (chili peppers) and rinse the cabbage quickly. Squeeze out excess moisture. Cut the cabbage into bite-size pieces and serve cold.
Serves 4 to 6
Note: the cabbage will keep, in the marinade, in the refrigerator for about 1 week.

Sunomono Daikon
White Radish Salad

METRIC/IMPERIAL	AMERICAN
1 white radish (daikon) about the size of a cucumber, peeled and finely grated	1 white radish (daikon) about the size of a cucumber, peeled and finely grated
4 tablespoons vinegar	¼ cup vinegar
2 tablespoons sugar	2 tablespoons sugar
pinch of salt	pinch of salt
⅕ cucumber, diced	⅕ cucumber, diced
1 persimmon, diced slightly larger than the cucumber	1 persimmon, diced slightly larger than the cucumber
1 teaspoon grated fresh horseradish	1 teaspoon grated fresh horseradish
1 teaspoon grated fresh root ginger	1 teaspoon grated fresh ginger root

Gently squeeze the radish in a cloth to remove the excess liquid. Mix together the vinegar, sugar and salt and add to the radish. Toss to coat. Add the remaining ingredients and mix well. Shape in mounds and place on plates.
Serves 4

Empress of the East Salad

METRIC/IMPERIAL	AMERICAN
¾ head of celery or Chinese cabbage (napa), torn into bite-size pieces	¾ head of celery or Chinese cabbage (napa), torn into bite-size pieces
100 g/4 oz spinach, torn into bite-size pieces	¼ lb spinach, torn into bite-size pieces
½ bunch of endive, chopped	½ bunch of curly endive (chicory), chopped
100 g/4 oz Gruyère cheese, cubed	¼ lb Swiss cheese, cubed
milk	milk
1 tablespoon toasted sesame seeds	1 tablespoon toasted sesame seeds
2 medium turnips, shredded	2 medium-size white turnips, shredded
few small tomatoes	few cherry tomatoes
Dressing:	**Dressing:**
2 tablespoons plain flour	2 tablespoons all-purpose flour
2 tablespoons brown sugar	2 tablespoons brown sugar
1 teaspoon ground ginger	1 teaspoon ground ginger
pinch of cayenne pepper	pinch of cayenne
1 teaspoon salt	1 teaspoon salt
1 egg, beaten	1 egg, beaten
250 ml/8 fl oz milk	1 cup milk
4 tablespoons white wine vinegar	¼ cup white wine vinegar
1 teaspoon butter	1 teaspoon butter
250 ml/8 fl oz soured cream	1 cup sour cream

First make the dressing: place the flour, sugar, ginger, cayenne and salt in a saucepan. Mix the egg with the milk, then gradually stir into the dry ingredients in the pan. Cook gently, stirring until thick and smooth. Gradually stir in the vinegar and butter. Remove from the heat and cool, then fold in the soured cream.

Place the salad greens in a large serving bowl and toss together. Dip the cubes of cheese in milk and then into sesame seeds to coat on all sides. Arrange the cheese cubes, turnips and tomatoes on the salad greens and serve with the dressing.
Serves 8

Yamazato Salad

METRIC/IMPERIAL	AMERICAN
salted jellyfish	salted jellyfish
1 cucumber, cut into fine shreds 4 cm/ 1½ inches long	1-2 cucumbers, cut into fine shreds 1½ inches long
1 carrot, cut into fine shreds 4 cm/ 1½ inches long	1 carrot, cut into fine shreds 1½ inches long
1 celery stick, cut into fine shreds 4 cm/ 1½ inches long	1 celery stalk, cut into fine shreds 1½ inches long
½ small lettuce, finely shredded	½ small head of lettuce, finely shredded
1 green pepper, cored, seeded and cut into fine shreds 4 cm/1½ inches long	1 green pepper, seeded and cut into fine shreds 1½ inches long
3 small onions, thinly sliced	3 small onions, thinly sliced
1 tablespoon white sesame seeds	1 tablespoon white sesame seeds

Dressing:

METRIC/IMPERIAL	AMERICAN
120 ml/4 fl oz light soy sauce	½ cup light soy sauce
6 tablespoons sweetened rice wine	6 tablespoons sweetened rice wine
4 tablespoons vinegar	¼ cup vinegar

Soak the jellyfish in cold water to remove salt for about 30 minutes. Drain and cut into thin strips. Pour a little hot water over the strips, then drain again and leave to cool.

Place all the vegetables in cold water and leave for 15 minutes to become crisp.

Heat the sesame seeds in a frying pan until they start to crack. Remove from the heat and cool.

Drain the vegetables and place them in a serving bowl. Top with the jellyfish and sesame seeds. Mix together the ingredients for the dressing and pour over the salad.
Serves 6

Carrot and Kidney Bean Salad

METRIC/IMPERIAL	AMERICAN
1 carrot, thinly sliced lengthways	1 carrot, thinly sliced lengthwise
24 canned red kidney beans	24 canned red kidney beans
salt	salt
4 tablespoons basic stock (page 12)	¼ cup basic stock (page 12)
50 g/2 oz sugar	¼ cup sugar
2 tablespoons light soy sauce	2 tablespoons light soy sauce
3 tablespoons white sesame seeds	3 tablespoons white sesame seeds
175 g/6 oz soy bean curd (tofu)	6 oz soybean curd (tofu)

Drop the carrot and kidney beans into boiling salted water and simmer just until the carrot is tender. Drain well and mix with the stock, 1 teaspoon sugar and 5 teaspoons of the soy sauce. Leave to cool.

Scatter the sesame seeds over the bottom of a frying pan and fry until they begin to crack. Remove from the heat and mix with 2 teaspoons of the sugar.

Cook the bean curd in boiling water until just tender, then drain well, pressing out excess water. Chop the bean curd and mix with the remaining sugar and soy sauce and ¾ teaspoon salt. Fold in the carrot and kidney beans and sprinkle over the sesame seeds.
Serves 4

Rice & Noodle Dishes

Hiyashi Somen
Chilled Noodles

METRIC/IMPERIAL	AMERICAN
450 g/1 lb thin wheat vermicelli (somen)	1 lb thin wheat vermicelli (somen)
450 ml/¾ pint basic stock (page 12)	2 cups basic stock (page 12)
120 ml/4 fl oz light soy sauce	½ cup light soy sauce
4 tablespoons rice wine	¼ cup rice wine
1 tablespoon sugar	1 tablespoon sugar
Garnish:	**Garnish:**
few ice cubes	few ice cubes
few small tomatoes, quartered	few small tomatoes, quartered
few spring onions, shredded	few scallions, shredded

Cook the noodles in boiling water for about 5 minutes or until just tender. Drain and rinse under cold running water. Drain well again and chill.

Put the stock, soy sauce, wine and sugar in a saucepan and bring to the boil. Simmer for 2 minutes. Cool, then pour into individual bowls. Chill.

Garnish the chilled noodles with ice cubes, tomatoes and spring onions (scallions) and serve with the sauce.
Serves 4

Tsukimi Udon
Noodles with Broth

METRIC/IMPERIAL	AMERICAN
450 g/1 lb thick broad noodles (udon)	1 lb thick broad noodles (udon)
900 ml/1½ pints basic stock (page 12)	1 quart basic stock (page 12)
1 tablespoon sugar	1 tablespoon sugar
1½ teaspoons salt	1½ teaspoons salt
1 tablespoon light soy sauce	1 tablespoon light soy sauce
4 eggs	4 eggs
Garnish:	**Garnish:**
2 spring onions, thinly sliced	2 scallions, thinly sliced
1 × 13 cm/5 inch square piece of dried seaweed, toasted and finely shredded	1 (5 inch) square piece of dried seaweed, toasted and finely shredded

Add the noodles to a large saucepan of boiling water. Bring back to the boil, then add 250 ml/8 fl oz cold water. Bring back to the boil again and cook for 10 to 12 minutes or until just tender. Drain and rinse thoroughly under cold running water. Drain well again.

Put the stock, sugar, salt and soy sauce in a saucepan and bring to the boil. Add the noodles and cook, stirring, until heated through. Pour into individual warmed bowls and break an egg into each. Cover the bowls, with lids if possible, so that the heat from the broth will cook the eggs.

Garnish with spring onions (scallions) and seaweed and serve hot.
Serves 4

Hiyashi Somen; Tsukimi Udon

Sekihan
Steamed Pink Rice with Beans

METRIC/IMPERIAL	AMERICAN
200 g/7 oz sweetened red beans (azuki), rinsed	¾ cup sweetened red beans (azuki), rinsed
750 g/1¾ lb glutinous sweet rice (mochigome), rinsed	4 cups glutinous sweet rice (mochigome), rinsed
1 teaspoon black sesame seeds	1 teaspoon black sesame seeds
2 teaspoons salt	2 teaspoons salt

Put the beans in a saucepan, cover with water and bring to the boil. Drain, cover with fresh water and bring to the boil again. Cover and simmer for about 40 minutes. Drain, reserving the cooking liquid.

Pour the cooking liquid over the rice and leave to stand overnight to allow the rice to turn pink.

Drain the rice, reserving the liquid. Mix the beans and rice together gently. Line a steamer plate with a piece of cheesecloth and spread the rice mixture on it. Pat it smooth and make a few vent holes in the rice mixture. Steam for about 50 minutes or until the rice is tender, basting every 12 minutes with the reserved bean cooking liquid.

Mix the sesame seeds with the salt. Sprinkle over the rice and beans and serve hot or at room temperature.
Serves 8 to 10

Sushi
Vinegared Rice

METRIC/IMPERIAL	AMERICAN
575 g/1¼ lb medium grain rice	3 cups medium grain rice
750 ml/1¼ pints water	3 cups water
6 tablespoons rice vinegar	6 tablespoons rice vinegar
4½ tablespoons sugar	4½ tablespoons sugar
2 teaspoons salt	2 teaspoons salt
1 teaspoon monosodium glutamate (optional)	1 teaspoon msg (optional)
1-2 tablespoons toasted sesame seeds to garnish	1-2 tablespoons toasted sesame seeds for garnish

Wash the rice thoroughly under cold running water until the rinsing water is clear. Drain in a colander for about 20 minutes.

Put the rice in a heavy saucepan, add the water, cover and bring to the boil. Lower the heat and simmer for 15 minutes. Remove from the heat and leave to stand for 20 minutes, without removing the lid.

Meanwhile put the vinegar, sugar, salt and monosodium glutamate, if using, in a saucepan and heat, stirring, until the sugar has dissolved. Set aside.

Fluff the rice with a fork, then transfer it to a stainless steel or ceramic bowl. Pour over the vinegar sauce and toss lightly together. Sprinkle with the sesame seeds and serve hot. Serves 4 to 6

Rice Salad

METRIC/IMPERIAL	AMERICAN
625 g/1 lb 6 oz steamed rice (right)	4 cups steamed rice (right)
1 × 425 g/15 oz can bean sprouts, drained	1 can (16 oz) bean sprouts, drained
2 sticks celery, sliced diagonally	2 stalks celery, sliced diagonally
½ green pepper, cored, seeded and diced	½ green pepper, seeded and diced
1 × 150 g/5 oz can water chestnuts, drained and sliced	1 can (5 oz) water chestnuts, drained and sliced
450 g/1 lb prawns, cooked, peeled and chopped	1 lb shrimp, cooked, shelled and chopped
4 tablespoons seasoned rice vinegar	¼ cup seasoned rice vinegar
4 tablespoons oil	¼ cup oil
4 tablespoons light soy sauce	¼ cup light soy sauce
2 spring onions, thinly sliced	2 scallions, thinly sliced

Place the rice, bean sprouts, celery, green pepper, water chestnuts and prawns (shrimp) in a bowl and fold together gently. Cover and chill for at least 30 minutes.

Mix together the vinegar, oil and soy sauce and pour this dressing over the salad. Add the spring onions (scallions) and toss well.
Serves 6

Nigiri Zushi
Rice Balls with Topping

METRIC/IMPERIAL	AMERICAN
1 tablespoon rice vinegar	1 tablespoon rice vinegar
575 g/1¼ lb vinegared rice (see left)	3 cups vinegared rice (see left)
1 tablespoon dry green horseradish (wasabi), mixed to a paste with water	1 tablespoon dry green horseradish (wasabi), mixed to a paste with water
30 small slices of raw fresh tuna or sea bass	30 small slices of raw fresh tuna or sea bass
parsley sprigs to garnish	parsley sprigs for garnish

Moisten the hands with a little vinegar. Scoop up about 2 tablespoons of the rice and squeeze into an egg-shaped oval, about 5 cm/2 inches long. Put a dab of the horseradish paste on top, then press on a slice of fish. Repeat, to make 30 rice balls.

Arrange the rice balls on a serving platter and garnish with parsley sprigs. Serve with light soy sauce for dipping.
Makes 30

Gohan
Steamed Rice

METRIC/IMPERIAL	AMERICAN
575 g/1¼ lb short or medium grain rice	3 cups short or medium grain rice
750 ml/1¼ pints water	3 cups water

Wash the rice thoroughly under cold running water until the rinsing water is clear. Drain in a colander for about 20 minutes.

Put the rice in a heavy saucepan, add the water, cover and bring to the boil. Lower the heat and simmer for 20 minutes or until most of the water has been absorbed. Increase the heat and cook for about 20 seconds, then remove from the heat and leave to stand for 10 minutes, without removing the lid.

Fluff the rice with a fork and serve hot.
Serves 4 to 6

Chestnut Rice

METRIC/IMPERIAL	AMERICAN
675 g/1½ lb medium grain rice	3½ cups medium grain rice
1 litre/1¾ pints water	1 quart water
2 tablespoons light soy sauce	2 tablespoons light soy sauce
1¼ teaspoons rice wine	1¼ teaspoons rice wine
½ teaspoon salt	½ teaspoon salt
24 chestnuts, peeled	24 chestnuts, peeled

Wash the rice thoroughly under cold running water until the rinsing water is clear. Drain in a colander for about 20 minutes.

Put the rice in a heavy saucepan and add the remaining ingredients. Cover and bring to the boil. Lower the heat and simmer for 20 minutes or until most of the water has been absorbed. Remove from the heat and leave to stand for 10 minutes, without removing the lid. Fluff the rice with a fork and serve hot.
Serves 6

Fried Rice

METRIC/IMPERIAL	AMERICAN
1 tablespoon oil	1 tablespoon oil
1 medium onion, finely chopped	1 medium-size onion, finely chopped
1 small green pepper, cored, seeded and chopped	1 small green pepper, seeded and chopped
1 small clove garlic, crushed	1 small clove garlic, crushed
575 g/1¼ lb steamed rice (left)	3 cups steamed rice (left)
1 egg, beaten	1 egg, beaten
2 tablespoons light soy sauce	2 tablespoons light soy sauce

Heat the oil in a frying pan. Add the onion, green pepper and garlic and fry until softened. Stir in the rice and heat through, stirring occasionally. Add the egg and soy sauce and cook, stirring, for 2 to 3 minutes or until the egg has set.
Serves 6

Desserts

Zenzai or Shiruko
Red Bean Soup with Rice Dumplings

METRIC/IMPERIAL	AMERICAN
225 g/8 oz sweetened red beans (azuki), rinsed	1 cup sweetened red beans (azuki), rinsed
1.5 litres/2½ pints water	1½ quarts water
275 g/10 oz sugar	1¼ cups sugar
½ teaspoon salt	½ teaspoon salt
½ packet glutinous sweet rice flour	½ package glutinous sweet rice flour

Put the beans and water in a saucepan and bring to the boil. Simmer for 2 hours or until the beans are tender.

Make the liquid up to the original quantity again and add the sugar and salt. Simmer for 5 minutes, stirring occasionally.

Meanwhile mix the rice flour with enough water to make a stiff dough. Knead well, then pinch off tiny portions and form into balls about the size of marbles. Make a small indentation in the side of each ball.

Bring the bean soup back to the boil, then drop in the dumplings. Cook until the dumplings rise to the surface. Serve hot.
Serves 4

Momo No Kanten
Peach Dessert

METRIC/IMPERIAL	AMERICAN
1 long block of seaweed 'gelatine' (kanten)	1 long block of seaweed 'gelatin' (kanten)
450 ml/¾ pint water	2 cups water
350 g/12 oz sugar	1½ cups sugar
120 ml/4 fl oz fresh peach pulp	½ cup fresh peach pulp
juice of ½ lemon	juice of ½ lemon
2 egg whites	2 egg whites

Put the gelatine in a saucepan, cover with the water and leave to soak for 20 to 30 minutes. Bring to the boil, stirring until completely melted. Add the sugar and stir until dissolved. Strain into a bowl. Stir in the peach pulp and lemon juice and leave to cool.

Beat the egg whites until stiff and fold into the cooked peach mixture. Pour into a shallow pan and chill until set. Cut into 2.5 cm/1 inch squares or diamond shapes to serve.
Makes about 24

Matcha Ice Cream
Green Tea Ice Cream

METRIC/IMPERIAL	AMERICAN
600 ml/1 pint vanilla ice cream, softened	1 pint vanilla ice cream, softened
1 tablespoon powdered green tea	1 tablespoon powdered green tea

Blend together the ice cream and tea, then freeze until required.
Serves 4

Matcha Ice Cream; Momo No Kanten

Almond Creams with Apricot Sauce

METRIC/IMPERIAL	AMERICAN
1 tablespoon gelatine, dissolved according to packet instructions	1 tablespoon unflavored gelatin
100 g/4 oz sugar	½ cup sugar
pinch of salt	pinch of salt
2 eggs, separated	2 eggs, separated
300 ml/½ pint milk	1¼ cups milk
½ teaspoon almond essence	½ teaspoon almond extract
250 ml/8 fl oz double cream	1 cup heavy cream
toasted flaked almonds to decorate	toasted slivered almonds for decoration
Sauce:	**Sauce:**
350 ml/12 fl oz apricot juice	1½ cups apricot nectar
100 g/4 oz sugar	½ cup sugar
1 teaspoon lemon juice	1 teaspoon lemon juice
75 g/3 oz dried apricots, chopped	½ cup chopped dried apricots

Place the gelatine, half the sugar, the salt, egg yolks and milk in a saucepan and heat gently, stirring, until the gelatine has completely dissolved and the mixture is smooth. Remove from the heat and stir in the almond essence (extract). Chill until the mixture is beginning to thicken.

Beat the egg whites until frothy, then gradually beat in the remaining sugar and continue beating until stiff and glossy. Whip the cream until thick. Fold the cream and egg whites into the egg yolk mixture. Divide between eight moulds, each with a 150 ml/¼ pint (⅔ cup) capacity. Chill until set.

To make the sauce, place all the ingredients in a saucepan, cover and simmer for 20 to 25 minutes or until the apricots are tender. Chill.

To serve, pour the sauce over the unmoulded almond creams and top with almonds.
Serves 8

Yokan
Red Bean Cakes

METRIC/IMPERIAL	AMERICAN
2 × 425 g/15 oz cans red kidney beans, drained	2 cans (16 oz each) red kidney beans, drained
450 g/1 lb sugar	4 cups sugar
2 tablespoons salt	2 tablespoons salt
1 long block of seaweed 'gelatine' (kanten)	1 long block of seaweed 'gelatin' (kanten)
450 ml/¾ pint water	2 cups water
1 egg white	1 egg white
2 tablespoons redcurrant jelly	2 tablespoons red currant jelly

Purée the beans in a blender or food processor or press through a sieve. Mix the bean purée with half the sugar and the salt, stirring until the sugar has dissolved.

Put the gelatine in a saucepan, cover with the water and leave to soak for 20 to 30 minutes. Bring to the boil, stirring until completely melted. And the remaining sugar and stir until dissolved. Strain the liquid and return to the pan. Add the bean paste, egg white and jelly and stir as if kneading. Boil the mixture down to a gluey, starchy residue. While still liquid, pour into a square metal pan. Leave to cool and set, then cut into rectangles. Chill before serving.

Tofu Ice Cream
Soy Bean Curd Ice Cream

METRIC/IMPERIAL	AMERICAN
500 g/1 lb 2 oz soy bean curd (tofu)	1 lb 2 oz soybean curd (tofu)
3 tablespoons honey	3 tablespoons honey
¼ teaspoon vanilla essence	¼ teaspoon vanilla extract
pinch of salt	pinch of salt

Place 350 g/12 oz of the bean curd, the honey, vanilla and salt in a blender or food processor and process for 1 minute or until smooth. Pour into a covered container and freeze overnight.

Purée the remaining bean curd until smooth. Break the frozen mixture into small chunks. Add, a few at a time, to the puréed bean curd processing at high speed. When all the frozen mixture has been added and the mixture is thick and smooth, the ice cream is ready to be served.
Serves 4

Kasutera
Sponge Cake

METRIC/IMPERIAL	AMERICAN
5 eggs	5 eggs
150 g/5 oz sugar	2/3 cup sugar
75 g/3 oz honey	1/4 cup honey
75 g/3 oz flour	3/4 cup flour
3/4 teaspoon baking powder	3/4 teaspoon baking powder
2 tablespoons icing sugar	2 tablespoons confectioners' sugar

Put the eggs in a bowl and beat lightly, then beat in the sugar and honey. Continue beating for about 10 minutes or until thick and pale, using an electric beater if possible.

Sift the flour and baking powder together and fold into the egg mixture. Pour into a greased and floured 23 cm/9 inch square cake pan. Bake in a preheated moderate oven (180°C/350°F, Gas Mark 4) for 30 minutes. Cool in the pan for 10 minutes, then transfer to a wire rack to cool completely. When cold, sprinkle over the icing (confectioners') sugar. Cut into pieces to serve.

Red Bean Buns

METRIC/IMPERIAL	AMERICAN
450 g/1 lb sugar	4 cups sugar
250 ml/8 fl oz water	1 cup water
350 g/12 oz flour	3 cups flour
1 teaspoon powdered green tea	1 teaspoon powdered green tea
2 × 425 g/15 oz cans red kidney beans	2 cans (16 oz each) red kidney beans
2 tablespoons salt	2 tablespoons salt

Put half the sugar in a bowl with the water and stir to dissolve. Sift the flour and tea into the bowl and mix to make a smooth dough.

Purée the drained beans in a blender or food processor, or press through a sieve. Mix the bean purée with the remaining sugar and the salt. Strain this bean paste.

Divide the dough into small portions and flatten each into a small round sheet. Shape the bean paste into small balls and place one ball in the centre of each dough sheet. Wrap the dough around the paste ball to enclose it completely. Steam the buns inside a wet cloth over boiling water for 15 minutes.

Tofu Fruit Whip
Soy Bean Curd Fruit Whip

METRIC/IMPERIAL	AMERICAN
350 g/12 oz soy bean curd (tofu), chilled	3/4 lb soybean curd (tofu), chilled
225 g/8 oz prepared strawberries, peaches or pineapple	1/2 lb prepared strawberries, peaches or pineapple
1 tablespoon honey	1 tablespoon honey
chopped nuts	chopped nuts

Place the bean curd, fruit and honey in a blender or food processor and process until smooth. Serve topped with chopped nuts.
Serves 4

Apple Gelatine

METRIC/IMPERIAL	AMERICAN
2 blocks of seaweed 'gelatine' (kanten)	2 blocks of seaweed 'gelatin' (kanten)
450 ml/3/4 pint water	2 cups water
450 ml/3/4 pint apple juice	2 cups apple juice
pinch of salt	pinch of salt
1/2 lemon, thinly sliced	1/2 lemon, thinly sliced
pinch of dried peppermint leaves	pinch of dried peppermint leaves
prepared fruit in season, such as strawberries, melon, pears (optional)	prepared fruit in season, such as strawberries, melon, pears (optional)

Put the gelatine into a saucepan, cover with the water and apple juice and add the salt, lemon slices and peppermint. Bring to the boil, stirring, and simmer until the gelatine has completely melted.

Strain into a bowl. Allow to cool slightly, then add the fruit, if using. Pour into a decorative mould and chill until set.
Serves 6

Glossary

Aburage – Fried soy bean cake
Agemono – Deep-fried food
Aji-no-moto – Monosodium glutamate, or 'taste powder'
Azuki – Red beans; sweetened azuki beans are available in cans, sweetened

Bancha – Coarse green tea
Beni-shoga – Red salt-preserved ginger

Daikon – Large white radish, usually carrot-shaped
Dashi – Basic stock made by steeping kelp seaweed and dried bonito fish in water

Enokidake – Mushrooms with long thin stems and tiny button tops, in bunches

Gobo – Edible burdock roots
Goma – Sesame seeds
Goma abura – Sesame seed oil
Goma jio – Salted sesame seeds
Gyoza skins – Round dough skins, like Chinese wonton

Hakusai – Celery or Chinese cabbage
Harusame – Soy bean noodles
Hashi – Chopsticks
Hijiki – Brown algae seaweed

Kabocha – Pumpkin, marrow (squash)
Kamaboko – Japanese fish cake
Kanten – Seaweed used as gelatine, like agar-agar
Kanpyo – Dried gourd
Karashi – Mustard
Kasu – Rice wine lees, sold in blocks
Katsuobushi – Dried bonito fish
Kinugoshi – 'Silk' soy bean curd
Kombu – Kelp seaweed
Konnyaku – Tuber root cake

Maguro – Tuna fish
Matcha – Powdered green tea
Matsutake – Type of mushroom that grows in pine forests
Mirin – Sweetened rice wine
Miso – Soy bean paste
Miso akamiso – Red soy bean paste
Miso shiromiso – White soy bean paste
Mochigome – Glutinous sweet rice
Mochiko – Glutinous sweet rice flour

Moyashi – Bean sprouts
Mushimono – Steamed food

Napa – Celery or Chinese cabbage
Nasu – Aubergine (eggplant)
Negi – Green onion, leek
Nimono – Boiled food
Nira – Chives, spring onion (scallion)
Nori – Dried seaweed; purple laver

Panko – Coarse breadcrumbs

Renkon – Lotus root

Sake – Rice wine
Saifun – Mung bean threads
Sansho – Leaves of bush used to garnish o season; also available powdered as Japanes pepper
Sashimi – Raw fish
Satsumaimo – Sweet Potato
Seri – Japanese parsley
Shichimi – Seven spice mixture
Shiitake – Type of large, flat, dark mushroom available fresh or dried; cultivated in oak logs
Shimeji – Tree oyster mushroom
Shirataki – Yam noodles, in transparen threads
Shoga – Ginger
Shoyu – Light soy sauce
Shungiku – Edible chrysanthemum leaves
Soba – Fine buckwheat noodles
Somen – Very thin wheat vermicelli
Su – Rice vinegar
Sudare – Bamboo mat
Sunomono – 'Vinegared things', or salad
Sushi – Vinegared rice

Takenoko – Bamboo shoot
Tofu – Soy bean curd
Tonkatsu sauce – Bottled thick brown sauce

Udo – Spikenard
Udon – Thick broad noodles

Wakame – Lobe leaf seaweed
Wasabi – Green horseradish, usually ground dry

Yakidofu – Grilled (broiled) soy bean curd
Yakimono – Grilled (broiled) food
Yuzu – Lemon

Index

Almond creams with apricot sauce 60
Apple:
Apple gelatine 61
Fried pork and apple balls 44
Asparagus – Prawns with asparagus 8
Aubergine – Mustard-pickled aubergine 50

Baked fish with eggs 22
Barbecued beef teriyaki 36
Bean curd soup 13
Beans with eggs 49
Beef:
Barbecued beef teriyaki 36
Beef fondue with mushrooms 37
Beef 'hash' 41
Beef and radish juice fondue 40
Beef salad 40
Beef teriyaki fondue 37
Beef and wine fondue 38
Meat with miso 35
Oriental steak strips 36
Steak with vegetables 35
Braised marinated duck 33
Braised salmon 18
'Brown sack' sushi 49
Buta teriyaki 42

Cabbage:
Cabbage pickles 52
Ham and cabbage salad 41
Carrot and kidney bean salad 53
Chawanmushi 28
Chestnut rice 57
Chicken:
Chicken in broth 27
Chicken deep-fried with seaweed 28

Chicken and eggs with rice 29
Chicken and mushroom cake 29
Chicken oharame 28
Chicken with prawns and vegetables 32
Chicken rice 29
Chicken skewers 30
Chicken stuffed cucumbers 30
Chicken stuffed pumpkin 33
Easy chicken and vegetable sushi 28
Fish with mushrooms and chicken 16
Hot chicken and egg soup 28
Marinated chicken legs 33
Peanut chicken 32
Chirashi-zushi 25
Chiri nabe 16
Clams:
Clams with onions 20
Grilled clams 20
Cod and pineapple kebabs 22
Courgette – Pork and courgette stew 45
Crab and cucumber with vinegar sauce 10
Cucumber:
Chicken stuffed cucumbers 30
Crab and cucumber with vinegar sauce 10

Dashi 12
Dressed turnips 48
Duck – Braised marinated duck 33
Dumplings – Fried 9

Easy chicken and vegetable sushi 28
Ebishinjo 10
Egg:
Baked fish with eggs 22
Beans with egg 49
Egg soup 12

Hot chicken and egg soup 28
Omelet spinach roll 8
Smoked fish omelets 24
Empress of the east salad 52

Fish:
Baked fish with eggs 22
Fish with mushrooms and chicken 16
Fish rice 21
Fish and soy bean curd 18
Fish stew 16
Fish and vegetable fritters 7
Poached fish with vegetables 20
Salt grilled fish 15
Simple marinated fish 15
Sliced raw fish 10
Smoked fish omelets 24
Steamed fish with ginger 18
Sweet and pungent fish 22
White fish chowder 13
Fried dumplings 9
Fried meat and vegetables 38
Fried pork and apple balls 44
Fried rice 57
Fried soy bean curd 48

Gingered pork stew 42
Gohan 57
Green tea ice cream 59
Grilled clams 20
Gyoza yaki 9

Ham:
Ham and cabbage salad 41
Ham with peas 41
Hamaguri yaki 20
Harusame soup 47
Hijiki to aburage 48

Hiyashi somen 55
Horenso tamago maki 8
Hot chicken and egg soup 28

Ice cream:
Green tea ice cream 59
Soy bean curd ice cream 60

Japanese vegetables with prawns 17

Kabuto-age 21
Kamo no tsukiyaki 33
Karibayaki 40
Kasutera 61
Kidney bean – Carrot and kidney bean salad 53
Kyuri to kani no sunomono 10

Lobster and vegetables in 'fried armour' 21

Mackerel – Tuna and mackerel with vegetables and rice 25
Marinated chicken legs 33
Marrow with fish sauce 17
Matcha ice cream 59
Matsutake dobin 16
Meat with miso 35
Miso shiru 12
Mizutaki 27
Momo no kanten 59
Mushrooms:
Chicken and mushroom cake 29
Fish with mushrooms and chicken 16
Prawn stuffed mushrooms 25
Tree oyster mushrooms 49
Mussels and onions 20

Napa no tsukemono 52
Nasu no karashi 50

Nigiri zushi 57
Niku no miso yaki 35
Nioroshi 18
Nizakana 18
Noodles:
  Chilled noodles 55
  Noodles with broth 55
  Vegetable, noodle
    and sesame
    salad 50
Nuta negi 8

Omelet spinach roll 8
Onions – Clams or
    mussels and onions
    20
Oriental pork strips 44
Oriental steak strips 36
Oyako domburi 29

Pea:
  Ham with peas 41
  Peas with egg 49
Peach dessert 59
Peanut chicken 32
Poached fish with
    vegetables 20
Poached scallops 20
Pork:
  Fried pork and apple
    balls 44
  Gingered pork stew
    42
  Oriental pork strips
    44
  Piquant pork and
    prawns with
    noodles 42
  Pork chops 45
  Pork and courgette
    stew 45
  Pork and green bean
    salad 45
  Pork skewers 42
Prawns:
  Chicken with prawns
    and vegetables 32
  Japanese vegetables
    with prawns 17
  Piquant pork and
    prawns with
    noodles 42
  Prawns with
    asparagus 8
  Prawns with spinach
    and water
    chestnuts 17
  Prawn stuffed
    mushrooms 25

Pumpkin – Chicken
    stuffed pumpkin 33

Radish:
  Beef and radish juice
    fondue 40
  White radish salad 52
Red bean buns 61
Red bean cakes 60
Red bean soup with
    rice dumplings 59
Rice:
  Chestnut rice 57
  Chicken and eggs
    with rice 29
  Chicken rice 29
  Fish rice 21
  Fried rice 57
  Rice balls with
    topping 57
  Rice salad 56
  Steamed pink rice
    with beans 56
  Steamed rice 57
  Tuna and mackerel
    with vegetables
    and rice 25
  Vinegared rice 56

Sakana nitsuke 20
Salmon:
  Braised salmon 18
  Salmon with sake
    lees 15
Salt grilled fish 15
Sashimi 10
Scallops – Poached 20
Seafood and
    vegetable salad 24
Seaweed:
  Chicken deep-fried
    with seaweed 28
  Seaweed with fried
    bean curd 48
Sekihan 56
Sesame spinach salad
    47
Shabu-shabu 37
Shake no kasuzuke 15
Shimeji 49
Shio yaki 15
Shrimp balls 10
Simple marinated fish
    15
Smoked fish omelets 24
Soboro donburi 41
Soups:
  Bean curd soup 13
  Bean soup 12

Egg soup 12
Hot chicken and egg
    soup 28
Red bean soup with
    rice dumplings 59
Spring rain soup 47
White fish chowder 13
Soy bean:
  Bean curd soup 13
  Bean soup 12
  Fish and soy bean
    curd 18
  Fried soy bean curd 48
  Soy bean curd
    fondue 9
  Soy bean curd fruit
    whip 61
  Soy bean curd ice
    cream 60
Spinach:
  Omelet spinach roll 8
  Prawns with spinach
    and water
    chestnuts 17
  Sesame spinach
    salad 47
Sponge cake 61
Spring onions with
    miso 8
Spring rain soup 47
Steak with vegetables
    35
Steamed fish with
    ginger 18
Steamed pink rice
    with beans 56
Stock 12
Sukiyaki 35
Sunomono daikon 52
Sushi 49; 56
Sweet and pungent
    fish 22

Tempura 7
Teppanyaki 38

Tofu:
  Tofu fruit whip 61
  Tofu ice cream 60
  Tofu 'steak' 48
Tonkatsu 45
Tree oyster
    mushrooms 49
Tsukimi udon 55
Tuna and mackerel
    with vegetables and
    rice 25
Turnips – Dressed 48

Urauchi shiitake 25

Vegetables:
  Chicken with prawns
    and vegetables 32
  Easy chicken and
    vegetable sushi 28
  Japanese vegetables
    with prawns 17
  Lobster and
    vegetables in 'fried
    armour' 21
  Poached fish with
    vegetables 20
  Seafood and
    vegetable salad 24
  Vegetable, noodle
    and sesame salad
Vinegared rice 56

Water chestnuts –
    Prawns with spinach
    and water chestnuts
    17
White radish salad 52

Yakitori 30
Yamazato salad 53
Yokan 60
Yudofu 9

Zenzai 59

The publishers would like to acknowledge the following photographers – Robert Golden: pages 11; 14; 26; 39; 51; 54 and 58. Paul Williams: page 46. Illustrations by Susan Neale.

Recipes for this book have been contributed by the Japan Trade Center, New York; Hotel Okura, Tokyo; Shinbashi Restaurant, New York; Marukan Rice Vinegar; US Rice Council; US National Marine Fisheries Service; Bird's Eye Frozen Foods; US National Live Stock and Meat Board; Sunkist Growers; Japan Air Lines.